27.45

The
Arab
Americans

By Joan Brodsky Schur

LUCENT
BOOKS®

THOMSON

™

GALE

San Diego • Detroit • New York • San Francisco • Cleveland • New Haven, Conn. • Waterville, Maine • London • Munich

Dedication:
For Ed and Sarah and with many thanks to Lauri Friedman, Christine Eickelman, and Karima Alavi.

LIBRARY OF CONGRESS CATALOGING-IN-PUBLICATION DATA

Schur, Joan Brodsky.
    The Arab Americans / by Joan Brodsky Schur.
        p. cm. — (Immigrants in America)
Includes bibliographical references and index.
Summary: Discusses the past and present political upheavals that drove Arab immigrants to American soil and their ultimate success.
    ISBN 1-59018-075-5
    I. Title. II. Series.

Printed in the United States of America

CONTENTS

FOREWORD

Immigrants have come to America at different times, for different reasons, and from many different places. They leave their homelands to escape religious and political persecution, poverty, war, famine, and countless other hardships. The journey is rarely easy. Sometimes, it entails a long and hazardous ocean voyage. Other times, it follows a circuitous route through refugee camps and foreign countries. At the turn of the twentieth century, for instance, Italian peasants, fleeing poverty, boarded steamships bound for New York, Boston, and other eastern seaports. And during the 1970s and 1980s, Vietnamese men, women, and children, victims of a devastating war, began arriving at refugee camps in Arkansas, Pennsylvania, Florida, and California, en route to establishing new lives in the United States.

Whatever the circumstances surrounding their departure, the immigrants' journey is always made more difficult by the knowledge that they leave behind family, friends, and a familiar way of life. Despite this, immigrants continue to come to America because, for many, the United States represents something they could not find at home: freedom and opportunity for themselves and their children.

No matter what their reasons for emigrating, where they have come from, or when they left, once here, nearly all immigrants face considerable challenges in adapting and making the United States

their new home. Language barriers, unfamiliar surroundings, and sometimes hostile neighbors make it difficult for immigrants to assimilate into American society. Some Vietnamese, for instance, could not read or write in their native tongue when they arrived in the United States. This heightened their struggle to communicate with employers who demanded they be literate in English, a language vastly different from their own. Likewise, Irish immigrant school children in Boston faced classmates who teased and belittled their lilting accent. Immigrants from Russia often felt isolated, having settled in areas of the United States where they had no access to traditional Russian foods. Similarly, Italian families, used to certain wines and spices, rarely shopped or traveled outside of New York's Little Italy, a self-contained community cut off from the rest of the city.

Even when first-generation immigrants do successfully settle into life in the United States, their children, born in America, often have different values and are influenced more by their country of birth than their parents' traditions. Children want to be a part of the American culture and usually welcome American ideals, beliefs, and styles. As they become more Americanized—adopting Western dating habits and fashions, for instance— they tend to cast aside or even actively reject the traditions embraced by their parents. Assimilation, then, often becomes an ideological dispute that creates conflict among immigrants of every ethnicity. Whether Chinese, Italian, Russian, or Vietnamese, young people battle their elders for respect, individuality, and freedom, issues that often would not have come up in their homeland. And no matter how tightly the first generations hold onto their traditions, in the end, it is usually the young people who decide what to keep and what to discard.

The Immigrants in America series fully examines the immigrant experience. Each book in the series discusses why the im-migrants left their homeland, what the journey to America was like, what they experienced when they arrived, and the challenges of assimilation. Each volume includes discussion of triumph and tragedy, contributions and influences, history and the future. Fully documented primary and secondary source quotations enliven the text. Sidebars highlight interesting events and personalities. Annotated bibliographies offer ideas for additional research. Each book in this dynamic series provides students with a wealth of information as well as launching points for further discussion.

Who Are the Arab Americans?

Of all the immigrant groups America is home to, Arab Americans are unique. One thing that distinguishes Arab Americans from most other immigrant groups is that they do not all come from one country, nor do they all practice one religion. While Italian Americans trace their roots to Italy, and Jewish immigrants identify themselves by their religion, Arab Americans come to America from a wide array of countries and practice many different faiths. To understand who Arab Americans are, it is important to know something about the homelands they left behind when they immigrated to America.

The Arab World

Arab Americans trace their ancestry to the Arab world. The Arab world extends from the Persian Gulf, west across northern Africa, to the Atlantic Ocean. From north to south it encompasses countries from Syria to Sudan. The Arab world includes some but not all of the countries called the Middle East and refers to a different region. The Middle East encompasses countries like Iran, Israel, and Turkey, which are not part of the Arab world.

When Arab immigrants first left their homes for America in the last decades of the nineteenth century, the Arab world was not divided into nations as we know them today. Instead most of it was part of the Ottoman Empire, which was ruled by the Turks. These early immigrants came from the Ottoman province of Greater Syria and thus in America came to be known as the Syrians.

At the end of World War I the Ottoman Empire was carved up by the European powers and divided into countries. Today the countries of the Arab world include Algeria, Bahrain, Egypt, Iraq, Jordan, Kuwait, Lebanon, Libya, Morocco, Oman, Qatar, Saudi Arabia, Sudan, Syria, Tunisia, United Arab Emirates, and Yemen. The Arab world also includes the West Bank of the Jordan River and the Gaza Strip, where Palestinians still struggle to establish their own nation independent of Israel. Most Arab Americans trace their roots to Egypt, Iraq, Jordan, Lebanon, Syria, and the region some call Palestine.

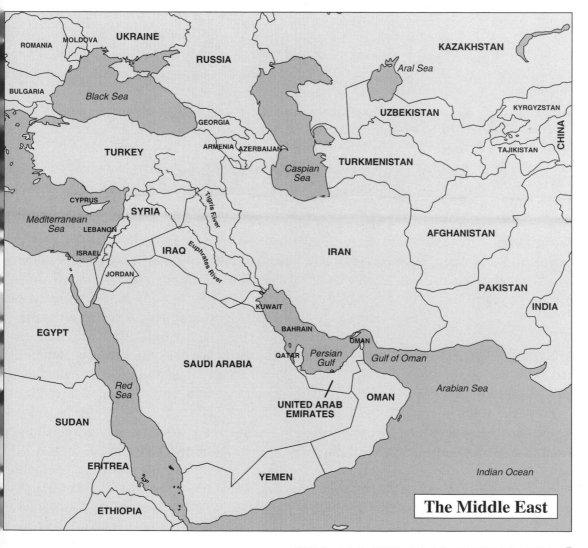

The Middle East

Defining Who Is an Arab

Many people assume, mistakenly, that all Arabs are Muslim and that most of the world's Muslims are Arabs. In fact, Arabs account for only 20 percent of the world's Muslim population. Also, not all Arabs are Muslim; many are Christian. One useful definition of an Arab is, "Arabs are those who speak Arabic as their native tongue and who identify themselves as Arabs."[1] Examples of people living in Arab lands who do not identify themselves as Arab are the Kurds, Jews, and Berbers.

Arabs share tastes in architecture, art, music, dress, and food. As well as speaking Arabic, Arabs hold in common similar values and traditions, and take pride in the glories of the Arab past, which include the Abbasid Empire (A.D. 749–1258), one of the high points of world civilization. Arab Americans brought many of these cultural traditions with them to America. They also transplanted their religions, which include a wide variety of both Christian and Muslim sects. In these ways, Arab Americans diversified the American landscape even while they themselves became a part of it.

A Small Group with an Important Role

Although Arab immigrants and their offspring have been coming to the United States since the late nineteenth century, Americans know surprisingly little about their Arab American neighbors. Arabs first arrived in relatively small numbers— about 124,000 came before 1924. They spread out quickly across the continent, dispersing their communities and thereby decreasing their visible presence. The early Arab immigrants also assimilated quickly, blending in so effectively that other Americans often overlooked their presence and many contributions to American life.

The second wave of Arab immigration, which began in the years following World War II, included many highly educated Arabs who prospered in America and in turn contributed to its prosperity. These immigrants, in addition to the first wave of Arab immigrants have made the Arab American population as a whole both wealthier and better educated than the average American.

Despite these successes, tragic events of the recent past have brought the Arab American community to the center of the public's attention, increasing the desire of many Americans to learn more about it. In the wake of turmoil in the Middle East, two wars in Iraq, and the terrorist attacks of September 11, 2001, Americans have had to confront their lack of knowledge and understanding about the Arab world and Islam, the world's second largest religion. Many Arab American organizations have seized this opportunity to help enlighten Americans about the world from which they came, and to teach Americans about the long and proud history of Arab Americans.

In recent years Arab Americans have been forced into the limelight in another way. After the terrorist attacks of September 11, America revised its immigration policies so that immigrants with ties to terrorist organizations would not gain entry to the United States. Other laws have tried to monitor the whereabouts of immigrants in the United States on temporary visas.

Thus far the new immigration laws have been applied exclusively to immigrants from Arab and Muslim countries. Some of the new policies have been challenged by civil rights groups, as well as Arab American organizations, which claim the new laws are discriminatory and unconstitutional. Arab Americans are thus in the forefront of a debate critical to America's future: how America can maintain its historic role as a beacon of hope to immigrants from around the world while keeping itself both a free society and a safe one.

CHAPTER ONE

The Syrian Pioneers: The First Wave

Today it is estimated that 3 million Americans trace their roots to an Arab country. While many Arab Americans are recent immigrants, most are the native-born descendants of Syrians who left their homelands in the Ottoman Empire beginning in the 1880s. This first wave of Arab immigration, which ended in the 1920s, was 90 percent Christian.

To reach America, travelers from the Middle East needed to cross the Atlantic Ocean, known in Arabic as "The Sea of Darkness." Arabs had plied the waters of the Mediterranean Sea and Indian Ocean for centuries, but these first settlers to America trod an unknown path across the Atlantic. Once here they encouraged other immigrants to follow in their wake. Between the 1880s and 1924, approximately 124,000 Arabic-speaking immigrants arrived on America's shores. All but a handful were Syrians—that is, they came from the Ottoman province of Greater Syria, a region that included modern-day Lebanon, Syria, Palestine, Israel, and Jordan. This was the generation that planted the seeds of Arab American life in America.

Economic Hardship in the Ottoman Empire

In the late nineteenth century, the Ottoman Turks ruled over most of the Arabic-speaking world, as they had for several centuries. The Ottomans were Muslims who ruled Syria from faraway Istanbul in Turkey. By the sixteenth century their empire ranged from eastern Europe to Africa, and included most of the Middle East. As the Ottomans pushed into central Europe, they confronted a variety of European countries, eager to see Ottoman power foiled. Gradually, the empire weakened as it came under attack from a variety of countries, and by the 1880s it had lost much of its territory. Despite efforts to modernize, the empire was in decline. Arabs in Greater Syria began to resent living under the Turks, who were unable to rule their empire effectively.

While Greater Syria was a relatively prosperous area of the Ottoman Empire, life was far from easy. Indeed, economic hardship was one reason Arabs left their homelands. Most of the population farmed. As the population of the district increased, however, there was less land to go around. Historian Alixa Naff writes, "Despite the cultivation of virtually every available inch of suitable land and the

Arab immigrant children pose for a photo in the early part of the twentieth century. Most of the first Arab immigrants to the United States were Syrian Christians.

prevalence of family gardens and private orchards, Mount Lebanon [a district of Greater Syria] was unable to produce enough to feed its population."[2] Episodes of drought and famine made life even harder.

Antonios Bishallany, the First Arab American

Antonios Bishallany was a Maronite Christian who led a brief but memorable life in America. Bishallany arrived in America in 1854, leading historians to believe he was the first Arab immigrant to settle there. He never intended to stay in America, but because he fell ill there, he never returned home. He died in 1856 only two years after his arrival.

Bishallany was born in Lebanon in 1827, where his family led a hard life. The family's vineyard and home were burned down by roaming thugs. To recover their losses, the family moved closer to Beirut, where Bishallany's father died when Antonios was only twelve years old.

Lebanon at this time was attracting many European tourists, eager to see the Holy Land. Other Europeans and Americans came to the Middle East as missionaries to convert Arabs to Roman Catholicism or Protestantism. Bishallany quickly found work as a tour guide and translator for the foreigners, and they in turn taught him about the world outside his homeland.

In 1854 Bishallany sold all of his possessions and boarded a ship for America. He knew no one from his homeland in America, but he did know many Americans whom he had previously taken on tour of the Holy Land. Soon he found work as a butler in the home of a wealthy New Yorker. Before long he was taking English lessons from New Yorkers who were eager to learn Arabic from him in exchange.

Bishallany was an intriguing figure to wealthy New Yorkers, who were fascinated by this foreigner from the unknown and exotic East. He dressed and spoke differently, but he knew how to ingratiate himself with Americans.

Bishallany wanted to improve his education while in America. One family helped him to attend a seminary school in upstate New York. His fellow students admired and liked this unusual young man, who was so eager to take advantage of everything America had to offer him. But soon, Bishallany fell ill with tuberculosis. His letters home attest to the fact that he knew he would die shortly.

Bishallany is buried in Green-Wood Cemetery in Brooklyn, where many illustrious New Yorkers of their day are also buried. He died far from home, without the companionship of friends or family from home. Today, not far from the cemetery, Atlantic Avenue bustles with the many Arab Americans who followed in Bishallany's wake to America.

By the latter part of the nineteenth century, much of the region's land was devoted to the growing of silk, further decreasing the land that was farmed. For many years the Mount Lebanon region had prospered through the sale of this cash crop, especially to Europeans. When the Suez Canal was built in 1869, however, Europeans found a more direct sea route to the Far East, where they preferred to buy silk. Adding to these difficulties, the Mount Lebanon region experienced a devastating silkworm blight, which destroyed many of the worms that naturally made silk. Considering that nearly half of all exports from Lebanon was silk, the Syrian industry was hit very hard.

In addition to hard times, people had to pay heavy taxes to the Ottomans. Although their taxes went to pay for police and law enforcement, many Arabs complained that these forces were not active in their communities and thus they resented the cost. The Arab American novelist Vance Bourjaily remembers how his grandmother resented paying taxes to their Turkish overlords:

> My grandmother spoke with a great deal of animosity of the Turks and particularly their tax-collecting methods. . . . [She told] stories about how her family outwitted them by hiding their assets when they got word from the next village that Turkish tax collectors were there. Sometimes her brothers would get in caves out in the hills and throw rocks at the tax collectors on their horses, try and scare them.[3]

Fleeing the Ottoman Draft

Young men also fled Greater Syria to avoid conscription (mandatory service) in the Ottoman army. In 1908 the Ottomans passed a new constitution granting members of all religions equal rights with Muslims. While this measure was intended to give greater freedom to the inhabitants of Ottoman lands, it had some unfortunate consequences for peoples of other faiths. Up until then, Jews and Christians had been exempt from conscription, but to compensate for the loss of their service they were forced to pay higher taxes. Now all Ottoman subjects, regardless of their faith, feared the draft.

Young men were torn from their families and villages. Parents had difficulty supporting themselves without the help of their young men. Because mortality rates in the Ottoman military were high, young men did whatever they could to avoid conscription. Some men hid in caves or even dressed as women to avoid being identified by the authorities and drafted. Others maimed themselves so they would be physically unfit for service. Emigration was yet another way out.

Fleeing Political Oppression

In the waning years of the nineteenth century, the residents of Greater Syria saw their political rights erode under Ottoman rule, and this became another reason they emigrated. For a brief period in the mid-nineteenth century the province had flourished. This was especially true of the Mount Lebanon region of Greater Syria, which the Ottomans had granted a large measure of autonomy. By the 1850s a thriving intellectual life took root there, and Beirut (the capital of what is now the nation of Lebanon) was its hub. Gathered around the city's universities, writers freely discussed politics and new ideas about democratic forms of government. A growing reading public devoured the many newspapers, magazines, and books written in Arabic.

Once they were free to read about political ideals taking root in Europe, the residents of Greater Syria yearned for greater freedom. France and Britain encouraged these desires. Eager to see the Ottomans lose control of their territory, many European powers encouraged some regions of the empire to demand their liberty and declare their independence from the Turks.

The Ottomans felt increasingly threatened by these developments. Thus, they cracked down on the free society that had flourished, taking away rights they had once granted. The newspapers that were spreading new ideas were promptly shut down, and severe punishments were established for anyone caught breaking the law. According to historian Najib E. Saliba, "Writers and journalists were subjected to imprisonment, fines and expulsion. Thousands of books were burned [by the Ottomans]."[4] In order to save books from the book burning, some people buried them in the ground so the authorities could not find them. Many intellectuals who escaped went first to Egypt, while others dreamed of greater freedom of expression in America.

World War I: New Reasons to Emigrate

During World War I, the Mount Lebanon region of Greater Syria suffered greatly. Britain and France blockaded the coastlines of the region as part of their efforts to defeat the Ottoman Empire. No ships carrying arms or food were allowed to enter or leave the ports for four years. This had devastating consequences for the population, leading to mass starvation of civilians.

The Ottomans supplied food for their army but did little to help the population. As food supplies dwindled, people were forced to eat weeds. The weakened population was soon prey to diseases, and before long there were outbreaks of yellow fever, typhoid, and dysentery. The blockade, however, prevented even medical supplies from reaching the region. In the Mount Lebanon region of Greater Syria, it is estimated that one hundred thousand died, a quarter of the population.

Religious Strife in the Ottoman Empire

Yet another thing that made life difficult in Greater Syria was the religious strife that afflicted the region in the nineteenth century. The Mount Lebanon region contained many sects of both Islam and Christianity. These groups, persecuted elsewhere, found refuge in the mountainous and inaccessible terrain of the area. Among the Christian Syrians, the largest groups were the Orthodox, Melchites, and Maronites. Among the Muslim sects in Mount Lebanon were the Druze, Alawis, and Ismailis.

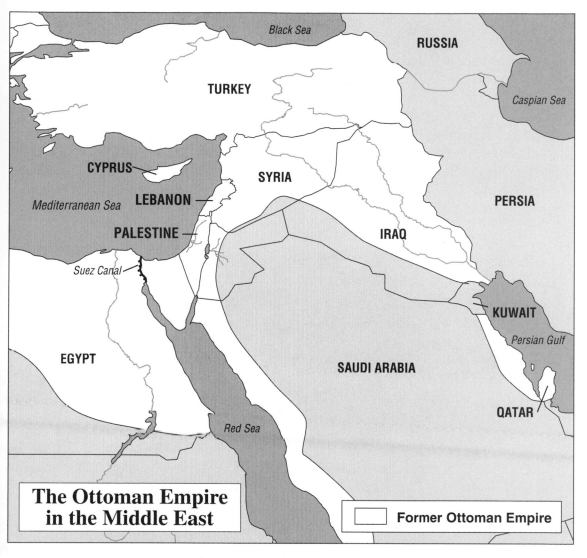

**The Ottoman Empire
in the Middle East**

Former Ottoman Empire

To govern their far-flung empire, the Ottomans divided their subjects into *millets*. *Millets* were essentially religious groups or sects, each one given leeway to govern themselves. While Jews, Muslims, and Christians practiced different faiths, they often lived and worked in small villages where they remained neighbors. Under this system there was little religious strife.

Religious turmoil began when Europeans arrived in the area. One way for Britain and France to gain a foothold in Ottoman lands was to claim that the empire's religious minorities needed European protection from the Muslim majority. For example, the French offered their aid to the Christian Maronites of Mount Lebanon, while the British took the Jews of Palestine under their wing.

Regardless of their particular faith, many Arabs often welcomed help from Europe. They wanted good trading partners, better schooling, and knowledge of Western farming techniques. Above all, the Arabs of Greater Syria hoped that the European countries would eventually help them overthrow their Ottoman rulers so that they could govern themselves.

However, by favoring some groups over others, Europeans created deep inequalities and anger among much of the populace. For example, with the help of France, the Maronites of Mount Lebanon began to prosper, moving into lands once held by the Muslim Druze. In 1840 fighting consequently broke out between the Druze and the Maronites. A truce was arranged, but it did not last. Finally in 1860 the Maronites attempted to push the Druze entirely out of Lebanon. The Druze retaliated, and horrific fighting broke out in what became known as the 1860 mas-

A Druze woman weaves a basket. Chronic conflict between Muslim Druze and Christian Maronites in nineteenth-century Lebanon caused many to flee the country.

sacres. Historian Gregory Orfalea writes of the 1860 massacres, "In a bloody twenty-two days, 7,771 Christians were murdered, 360 villages destroyed, 560 churches ruined, 43 monasteries burned, and 28 schools leveled. . . . Historians agree that because of the Druze-Christian disturbances, 1840–1860 were the two darkest decades in Syria since the Ottoman Turks captured the area in the sixteenth century."[5] Many Druze perished as well.

The Ottomans did nothing to prevent these massacres because they believed it was to their advantage to let their subjects fight against one another, rather than join forces against the Ottomans. Indeed, some observers believed the Ottoman Turks sought to escalate the violence. One survivor wrote:

> We had suffered from the Turks all our lives and had come to accept their methods of taking everything from us and giving us nothing in return but harsh words and more taxes. In 1860, however, there was a climax. The Druses hated us Christians and used to raid us every once in a while. That year the Turks urged them on us. . . . For three days the men and women of our village fought back. . . . They killed a good many of our neighbors before we fled.[6]

The Christians Leave First

The Christians' attempts to dominate the Druze of Mount Lebanon had backfired in terrible violence. Even though the fighting eventually subsided, the 1860 massacres left a residue of fear, especially among the Christians. Overall, the Christians were a minority in the Arab world, and many began to yearn for a predominantly Christian country to call home.

Many Muslims also wanted to leave, but they were less certain they would be welcomed in America. They did not know if they could retain their religious practices outside Dar al Islam, the realm of Islam. Some feared they would be persecuted for their beliefs. When Muslims first emigrated from Greater Syria, they often left for Egypt or another Muslim country instead of America. This helps to explain why 90 percent of the first wave of Arab immigrants to America were Christians, while only 10 percent were Muslim.

American Missionaries Spread the Word

Arabs first learned about America through the many foreign travelers who arrived in Greater Syria throughout the nineteenth century. These included archaeologists there to dig among the ancient ruins, biblical scholars who came to study in the Holy Land, painters, writers, and a growing number of tourists. The first sustained contact that Arabs had with Americans, however, was through the Protestant missionaries who flocked to the region. The missionaries hoped to convert Muslims to Christianity. While they did not have much success converting Muslims, they did succeed in igniting the dream of immigrating to America, especially among Christians.

The missionaries opened schools and universities. In 1866 they founded the Syrian Protestant College, which later became

The Arabic Language

One thing all Arabs have in common is that they speak Arabic. Like Hebrew, Arabic is a Semitic language written from right to left. Both Arabic and Hebrew share common roots in Aramaic. For example, the Hebrew word for "peace" is *shalom*, while in Arabic it is *salaam.*

The Koran, the Muslim holy book, was the first book to be written in Arabic. According to Islamic tradition, the prophet Muhammad received the first verses of the Koran in A.D. 610. They are believed by Muslims to be the word of God. For this reason great care was taken to preserve the Koran exactly as Muhammad received it—in Arabic. The spread of Islam and the Arabic language went hand in hand.

As the Arabs expanded into Africa, Asia, and Europe, Arabic became the means of communication across many cultures, just as Latin functioned in Christian Europe. It was the language of Islam, the language of great poetry, and the language in which scholars wrote to share their discoveries over a wide geographical area, whether they were Muslim, Jewish, or Christian. Arabic calligraphers took pains to transcribe the Koran in some of the world's most beautiful calligraphy.

Today, there are many spoken dialects of Arabic. Depending on where Arabic speakers are from, it can be either easy or difficult for them to understand one another. Among Americans today there is a renewed interest in many Arabic forms of poetry, as well as an increased desire to learn Arabic.

---

the American University of Beirut, one of the premier universities in the Middle East. They also established secondary schools to increase literacy and facilitate the reading of the Bible. As more people learned to read, knowledge of America was spread throughout the reading public.

Over time Christian Arabs, as well as some Muslim and Druze, took advantage of these schools to educate their children. At school, students were exposed to American values and attitudes. This made them both more eager to emigrate and better equipped to deal with life in America when they arrived.

One Syrian immigrant told the historian Philip Hitti: "The teacher in an American mission school had a great many pictures of American cities, streets and scenes, and I could see that life in that land was very different from ours. I heard about the telephone, telegraph and railroad, and as I already knew about ships on account of seeing them go by on the water, it began to dawn on me that there was a very great and active land outside of Mt. Lebanon."[7]

The missionaries also brought medical care to the region that was better than that of the Ottomans, and they founded hospitals that could cure a greater array of ailments. When famine, drought, or war devastated the region, the missionary hospitals raised money and donated what they could to the needy. All of these accomplishments made a favorable impression on the Arab population about the good-heartedness of Americans.

The American Expositions

Some Arabs first heard about America from those who returned from the Centennial Exhibition of 1876 in Philadelphia, which marked the one hundredth anniversary of the United States. To celebrate, America invited exhibitors from all over the world to display their wares on fairgrounds in Philadelphia.

The Ottoman sultan, Abdul Hamid II, encouraged Arab tradesmen and artisans to travel to America to display the glories of his empire. They brought with them coffee and spices, cotton and carpets, gold and porcelain, all of which they set up in elaborate displays. Their efforts were well rewarded. Historian Gregory Orfalea writes that "the Arabs and Turks, who won 129 awards, sent 1,600 individuals and firms, more than any other exhibitors except

the British and the United States itself."[8]

While Americans were impressed by the handiwork of the Orient, the Arab craftsmen were smitten by the technological marvels America showed off to the world at the fair. In Machinery Hall was the gigantic fifteen-hundred-horsepower

A replica of the Statue of Liberty's torch was featured at the 1876 American Centennial in Philadelphia, which hundreds of Arab exhibitors attended.

Corliss steam engine, as well as inventions such as the sewing machine, the steam-powered loom, and machines to speed the production of everything from wallpaper to newspapers.

The world was changing and the Arab visitors were impressed. Some stayed on in America after the Centennial Exhibition of 1876. More Arabs came to America for the international fairs that followed—in Chicago in 1893 and St. Louis in 1906. In letters to friends and relatives, these sojourners marveled at all that they had seen, sparking interest and curiosity about America in their homelands. When they returned home with their newly purchased leather shoes, gold watches, and American-style suits, they created a desire in many other Arabs to come to America.

The Dream Is Planted

This first glimpse of a better life in America coincided with hard times in Greater Syria. Many dreamed that they would go from rags to riches if only they could get to America. Historian Evelyn Shakir writes, "It was as if a door had suddenly swung open or been carelessly left ajar and through it people caught glimpses, highly colored as a postcard, of storybook places whose inhabitants led privileged

lives and where they, though newcomers, could earn more money than they had ever seen."[9]

Typical of the first immigrants to leave Greater Syria was Evelyn Shakir's grandfather, Jiryas. About him she writes,

He wanted to see America. Sometime in the late 1880s or early 1890s, the idea was planted, perhaps by his sister, who kept house for an American educator living in Beirut. Or perhaps the idea took root as Jiryas saw men he knew returning from the West [America] with enough money in their pockets to build fine houses with red-tiled roofs. . . . At any rate, flight must have been a daily temptation, since from his tiny house in his tiny village, he had a spectacular view of Beirut harbor, glistening blue and silver, traversed by ships that people said were bound for the United States.[10]

Like so many immigrants from Greater Syria, Jiryas decided to make the journey, leaving behind him his old life to begin a new one in America. Life in Greater Syria had grown too difficult, and the allure of America too great, to resist braving the unknown any longer.

CHAPTER TWO

Settling and Peddling

The first Arab emigrants to leave for America were unmarried men with little education and few skills who were willing to work hard. To finance the journey from Greater Syria, they mortgaged their property or borrowed from relatives. Some also paid for the trip by arrangement with the steamship companies who footed the cost of the journey in exchange for the immigrant's wages once he arrived. Many of these first sojourners hoped to stay in America for only a few years, get rich quickly, and return home with their profits. The vast majority, however, stayed on in America.

Momentum quickly built as more and more Arabs from Greater Syria left for America. The historian Samir Khalaf writes, "By the early 1890s the movement began to assume large proportions. Close to twenty-five hundred immigrants had entered the United States by 1891. By that time, every village in Lebanon could claim at least one immigrant son. By the late 1890s the exodus almost doubled."[11]

Having a family member established in America made it easier for those who followed to find work and a place to live. Some unmarried men returned to their homelands to find a wife to bring back to

What to Call the Immigrants from Greater Syria

In the early years of Arab immigration to America, the inspectors at Ellis Island did not know what to call the immigrants from Greater Syria. Until the Ottoman Empire collapsed at the end of World War I, immigrants from Greater Syria carried passports from the Ottoman Empire. For this reason the Ellis Island inspectors often counted them as "Turks," a name they resented, since the Turks were their oppressors. Later they were designated "Asiatic Turks" or "Turks from Asia." For this reason it is difficult for historians to know exactly how many immigrants from Arab lands came to America before the collapse of the Ottoman Empire at the end of World War I.

Adding to this confusion is the fact that the first wave immigrants did not necessarily think of themselves as Arabs either. If asked, the first wave immigrants probably would have identified themselves as members of a particular village or family clan. At this time in history the term *Arab* was much more selective than it is today, referring only to the nomadic Bedouin tribes of Arabia, who were Muslim. Nor did these immigrants identify themselves by nationality, since the countries we know of today in the Middle East did not yet exist. The best solution was to call the immigrants from the Ottoman province of Greater Syria *Syrians*, and this is how they referred to themselves in America.

America with them. Increasingly, whole families immigrated together. By 1910 close to a third of all Syrians in America were women, a relatively high proportion compared with many other immigrant groups.

While most of the first wave immigrants were illiterate villagers, educated professionals came as well. Some were graduates of the colleges established by Protestant missionaries in Mount Lebanon. They often came to further their studies in America. Syrian immigrant Dr. Ibrahim Arbeely, for example, was already a doctor when he arrived in America in 1878.

Journey to America

By the turn of the century, steamships had made the journey to America faster and safer than it had been in the days of sailing vessels. Beirut was ideally situated on the shores of the Mediterranean Sea, and European companies ran regular steamship service in and out of the city. From Beirut the steamships traversed the length of the Mediterranean Sea and passed through the Straits of Gibraltar to the Atlantic Ocean, which they crossed to reach America.

While at times the Ottomans forbade their citizens to emigrate, it was not difficult to get around these regulations. Immigrants simply bribed the corrupt Ottoman officials, who were always eager to supplement their meager salaries. The steamship companies were greedy, too. They actively recruited passengers and took their money, sometimes lying to the immigrants about where the ship was bound. When a Syrian disembarked, he might find himself in Mexico, Canada, or South America instead of America.

Because the immigrants had little money to pay for better accommodations, they traveled in steerage, where they were packed into tight and often unsanitary spaces. Although steamships weathered the ocean better than sailing vessels, storms and strong winds made the journey on "The Sea of Darkness" unpleasant at best and terrifying at worst. As New York Harbor and the Statue of Liberty came into view, the immigrants knew they had only one more hurdle to cross before they could disembark for America: making it through the inspection process at Ellis Island.

Arrival in America

The immigration station at Ellis Island was built in 1892 to accommodate the millions of immigrants from all over the world who were streaming into America at the turn of the century. Only those deemed acceptable by the inspectors were permitted to leave Ellis Island and enter for New York City and points beyond.

Most newcomers arrived with little money and no knowledge of English. Their greatest worry was that they would be deported. While the vast majority of immigrants were granted entry into the United States, the fear of being turned away made the inspection process a terrifying one.

A variety of officials examined the newcomers to determine if they were fit to stay in America. Inspectors inquired if immigrants had a criminal record in their home country. Doctors examined the immigrants to determine whether they were insane or sick, or otherwise unable to earn a livelihood in America. Immigrants who were afflicted with trachoma (a contagious eye infection) were immediately deported. Everyone feared being separated from their loved ones who were permitted to stay while they were forced to make the long journey in reverse.

Many things about America impressed the newcomers upon landing. The huge bridges, the elevators taking people straight up and down, the subways and telephones, the multitude of electric appliances in the home—these were some of the things that immigrants noted. New York City was unlike the cities of the Middle East in another important respect: the grid pattern on which the streets were laid out, making each street either parallel or perpendicular to every other. This was very different from the circuitous and narrow streets of the *madinas*, or city centers, of the Middle East.

Settling and Peddling

With the aid of a map and their own ingenuity, the Syrians quickly found their way around New York City, establishing their first communities on the Lower West Side of Manhattan and in Brooklyn. By 1921 half of the Syrian-born population of the United States lived in New York City. At first they rented rooms in boardinghouses and became pack peddlers, traveling salesmen who carried everything they sold in a bundle. Pack peddling was a trade that the Syrians probably learned from the Jewish immigrants on the Lower East Side, who pack peddled before they moved on to more lucrative lines of work.

Peddling was an ideal way to get started in America, even though it was very hard work. An industrious peddler could earn twice the weekly wages of a factory worker, and many preferred being out in all kinds of weather to being stuck inside a factory from dawn to dusk. Sturdy legs were a requirement, but it was not necessary to know English. A peddler needed no money to get started because he would get his wares on loan from a supplier, who was usually a former pack peddler himself. Then the peddler would be off selling his goods from house to house.

Christian Arabs predominated in this field because Muslim immigrants, already in a strange land, felt ill at ease in the homes of non-Muslims, and Muslim men were expected to avoid the company of women who were not family members. The Christian Arab peddlers often tried to impress their clients by telling them that the Christian crosses, religious statues, and holy water they sold came straight from the Holy Land, when in fact many items were made locally. Soon the trade included many other items as well. Historian Alixa Naff writes, "Peddling was ini-

tially a trade in rosaries, jewelry, and notions [buttons, ribbons] that would fit into a small case. It soon expanded into suitcases filled with a wide range of dry goods from bed linens to lace—almost anything that an isolated farmer's wife or housebound city dweller might want to buy."[12]

Peddling had other advantages as well. Americans who wanted to buy goods from the peddlers welcomed them into their homes to transact business. Here was the ideal opportunity for the Syrian immigrants to see how Americans lived, and to assess what goods they needed. Those who followed the trade learned a great deal about American life in the process. This helped the Syrians to assimilate more quickly than other immigrant groups who rarely ventured outside their own communities.

Some peddlers moved up in life by becoming the suppliers of goods to other peddlers. The suppliers performed many functions for the community. They became its informal bankers, extending credit to new peddlers and banking their money for them. Suppliers would also arrange the peddlers' routes and rent them rooms. While the relationship was an informal one, and peddlers could quit at any time, the suppliers were respected for their leadership skills. In the process the suppliers learned many of the things required of a boss, such as how to deal with local authorities and follow rules and regulations. These skills could be applied to other enterprises. This was fortunate because beginning in the early twentieth century, the peddling trade died out as retail stores became more common.

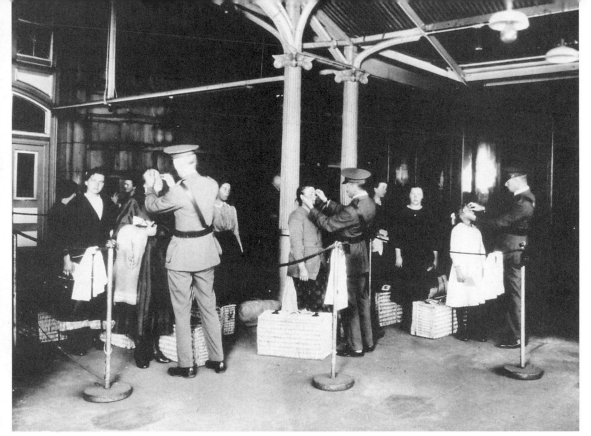

Immigration officials inspect newly arrived immigrants at Ellis Island around 1900. Most early Arab immigrants remained in New York City.

Moving on to New Enterprises

From peddling, many of the early Arabs in the New York City area moved into the sewing trades, as did their fellow peddlers, the Jews. The sewers, or needle workers as they were called, also produced sweaters, rugs, and fabrics. As they began to prosper, some Arabs opened silk factories in Manhattan and New Jersey. Silk was a valued commodity and a familiar one; the first wave immigrants had grown and processed it in the Mount Lebanon region of Greater Syria. By 1924 there were twenty-five Arab-owned silk factories making fancy and exotic goods. Rather than producing goods, other immigrants opened businesses importing goods from

the homelands, such as valuable Oriental carpets.

Many former peddlers became grocery store owners as they put down roots in the big and small cities to which they traveled. These were often mom-and-pop stores, small family-run shops that in a tiny space sold all the basic necessities. They were usually open night and day, employing many family members in the process.

One advantage of being the owner of such a store was that you could hire whom you wished: your relatives. In fact the very purpose of opening such a store was often to provide jobs for newly arrived family members. "Initially immigrants

Arab immigrants shop in an Arab-owned grocery in New York City in the early 1900s. Many Syrian immigrants became grocery store owners.

became grocers because it was an available occupation, and not too difficult to learn. Before long, however, new immigrants were becoming grocers for an additional reason, the desire to work with relatives,"[13] writes historian Mary C. Sengstock. Sometimes whole villages gradually immigrated to America this way, thus establishing "Little Syrias" in their new country.

Craving the foods they ate in their homelands, many Arab Americans opened restaurants. These restaurants introduced Middle Eastern cuisine to America. They served dishes like falafel (fava beans and spices fried to a crisp), hummus (a dip made of sesame seed paste and chickpeas), and sweets like baklava, which drips with honey. Soon Americans of all walks of life were enjoying these tantalizing foods as well.

Some enterprising grocery and restaurant owners moved on to work in the wholesale food industry, supplying other stores with goods. With the growth of chain supermarkets, food distribution became a big business in America, and Arab Americans were well situated to take advantage of this.

Women and Work

In Greater Syria, Arab women traditionally worked in the home. Fortunately for Syrian American women, most of the work assumed by their male relatives in the United States was also deemed appropriate for women. Male shop owners often worked below their homes, so that women could easily watch their families and help out at the family grocery or dry goods store at the same time. A Lebanese woman recounted how she raised her children while working: "I used to work . . . day and night. When I get my son, Joe, I put him in the carriage. When he cry, I shake the carriage with my feet and work with my hands."[14] Peddling, work in textile factories, and garment making were all considered acceptable jobs for women in America, provided other women or male family members were with the women to protect their safety and honor.

Women made hardy peddlers. As Alixa Naff recounts, "The more enterprising and determined . . . remained on the road for weeks or months at a time, covering several states. . . . Most women, children, and old people remained within range of the settlement to which they returned in the evening. In addition to peddling, many women crocheted, embroidered, and sewed goods at home for their menfolk to sell."[15]

Immigrant Hannah Shakir, who settled in Boston, recounts, "Many of the women went peddling, carrying a big bag with

The Syrian Ladies' Aid Societies

In the early twentieth century, Arab women were not expected to work outside the home. This was true whether they were Christians or Muslims. Once in America, the role of women began to change because their earning power was often necessary to the survival of their families.

One outlet for women with energy and drive was to join the Syrian ladies' aid societies that sprouted up in a variety of American cities. Women organized the first aid societies during World War I as a way to raise money for desperate relatives suffering from the effects of war and famine in the homelands. Later their work focused on providing a safety net of services for Syrian immigrants, such as providing milk, coal, or arranging medical care for needy families. Fund-raising efforts took persistence and skill, bringing women together in a community of warmth and support as they planned picnics, rummage sales, and bazaars or visited homes and hospitals.

The importance of these clubs dwindled as the first wave immigrants assimilated and as the U.S. government passed social legislation that provided families with government-sponsored support like social security and unemployment benefits. Still the clubs persisted into the 1960s and beyond. As more women entered the professions in the years following the feminist movement of the 1970s, some ladies' aid societies raised money to help send women of Arab American descent to college.

lots of merchandise—laces, thread, stockings. They went from door to door carrying the bags on their shoulders and taking the streetcars wherever they went. They didn't know how to read the signs on the cars, so they went by the colors. This color car goes to Cambridge, this color to Chelsea."[16]

Some women with a keen eye for good taste sold elegant luxury silks and embroidered goods to wealthy women. One such woman bragged that all her New England customers were "Big people . . . multi-multi-millionaires!"[17] Marie Azeez El-Khoury, who emigrated from Mount Lebanon when she was five, inherited her father's jewelry business and turned it into a world-class establishment on New York City's Fifth Avenue.

Other less fortunate women went to work in the textile mills of New England. After pack peddling, Hannah Shakir went

Many Arab Americans have succeeded in business. Jacques Nasser (pictured) became CEO of Ford Motor Company in the 1990s.

to work in the mills of Fall River, Massachusetts. She recalls of this experience,

> I worked in the biggest textile mill in Fall River. We made gingham [a cotton cloth]. I learned how to operate the looms, six big looms, just like a man. I did it very well. The looms ran by themselves, but when one stopped, I'd go and examine it to see what was wrong. . . . But it was hard work. When I first started, we used to work twelve hours a day, from six in the morning til six at night. And on Saturdays, til twelve.[18]

Historical records show that in Fall River, if a Syrian female was not married like Hannah Shakir, she most likely worked in the textile mills.

Spreading Out

While Arab Americans first settled along the eastern seaboard, it was peddling that sent them wandering all over America. Horses, wagons, and eventually cars allowed the peddlers to carry ever more wares to greater distances. As suppliers left their bases in northeast cities, they gradually clustered in other cities farther west. As the Arab immigrants moved west, they discovered the industrial heartland of America and began settling in cities like Pittsburgh and New Castle in Pennsylvania; Detroit, Michigan; and Michigan City, Indiana. In such places they went to work in the booming steel and auto industries, which were transforming America into an industrial giant of the twentieth century.

The first to arrive in Detroit were the Christians, principally the Syrian Orthodox and Maronites, as well as the Iraqi Chaldeans, but within ten years their Muslim compatriots followed. Gregory Orfalea writes, "Many of the first mass-produced autos were built by the olive-skinned hands of the early Syrian Muslims. So were the elegant, velvet-lined Pullman cars [for trains] in Michigan City."[19] Through the 1920s the auto industry was booming, providing jobs and financial security for the newcomers.

The Druze, less inclined to do factory work, sometimes tried their hand at farming. They settled in Appalachia and as far away as California and Washington. For the main part, however, the Arab immigrants were urban dwellers. By 1915 more than fifty American cities could boast thriving Arab American communities.

Becoming American

Arab American communities in the bigger cities came to be known as "Little Syrias" because they retained certain features of the homeland, such as traditional foods, festivals, and celebrations. However, the first wave Syrian pioneers did not develop as strong an ethnic identity as did other immigrant groups. Relative to other groups, the numbers of Syrian Americans in the first wave were small—under 150,000 in all. By contrast 4 million Italians arrived in America during the same time period.

Not only were there few Arabs overall, they were further subdivided by the great number of religious traditions they practiced within Christianity and Islam, and

Arab American Publications

As Arab Americans assimilated into life in America, it was important for them to keep up on news from their homelands. They did this through newspapers geared toward the Arab American community. At first, Arabic newspapers targeted specific subgroups within the Arab American community. For example, *Al-Hoda* was written for the Maronites, while *Meraat al-Gharb* addressed the Syrian Orthodox community. Writing for so many audiences split the readership until the 1930s when there were perhaps fifty papers, each catering to a small number of readers and competing against one another. Another fifty had already gone in and out of print because there were just too many publications for the number of readers. This impeded the community's ability to forge a sense of shared identity.

The *Syrian World*, first published in 1926, helped to unite the Arab American community. It was the first newspaper written in English. Because it targeted as its audience all Arab Americans, it reached a much wider readership. The *Syrian World* kept its subscribers abreast of developments in their native countries while encouraging them to adapt to American lifestyles. In her book *Becoming American: The Early Arab Immigrant Experience*, historian Alixa Naff writes, "Many Syrian immigrants, for the first time, became informed about the society, politics, history, literature, and culture of Arabs in general and Syria in particular. . . . Never before had these predominantly village-centered, unschooled readers learned so such about their heritage."

The *Syrian World* helped raise literacy rates as well as foster a sophisticated literary taste among its readers. Talented men and women, including poets and intellectuals, were encouraged to write for it. With the economic hardships of the Depression, however, the *Syrian World* went out of print.

Today immigrants in large cities can buy Arabic newspapers that are published in a variety of foreign countries or purchase magazines published in English, like *Arab American Business Magazine.* On the Internet Arab Americans can find a publication specifically aimed at their entire community. *Café Arabica* (www.cafearabica.com) was established in 1996. In her essay that appears in *A Community of Many Worlds: Arab Americans in New York City*, translator Inea Bushnaq writes, "It carries cultural and political news, announcements of events, interviews, profiles, book reviews, classified ads, job offers, travel tips, and a *souk* [marketplace], which, like the peddlers of old, brings a selection of wares, from books to foodstuffs, delivering them all from desktop to desktop."

by the many different regions of Greater Syria from which they came. Living in small groups, and spread far and wide across America, it was hard for them to retain their own cultures and easier to become absorbed into the American mainstream. Outside the major cities like New York, Chicago, and Detroit, their small and prosperous communities often went unnoticed by other Americans.

In some respects the Arabs were happy to go unnoticed: it meant they blended in with other Americans. In terms of politics, they kept a low profile, for the most part preferring not to draw attention to themselves. Some joined the labor movement, fighting for better wages and job security in the industries in which they worked. Others fought hard to raise America's awareness of the plight of the Arabs in their homelands, especially during the wartime famine of World War I. In general, however, the newcomers preferred not to call attention to themselves.

One explanation for the Arab reluctance to get involved in politics in America is that they had little experience doing so in their homelands. The Ottoman authorities were inept and remote from the people. Administrators in the homelands were often corrupt and contemptuous of the peasants they ruled. Even if an Arab complained to the authorities or tried to influence Turkish policy, nothing was likely to improve as a result. In fact, the person who stuck his neck out might just get in trouble. Political scientist Michael Suleiman believes that "the early Arab community in the United States often confused 'good citizenship' with avoidance of political activity, especially when such activity involved a challenge to specific laws or opposition to authority figures."[20]

Even the common use of the Arabic language could not hold together the far-flung Arab American community. As Arabs began to assimilate, the use of Arabic was largely forgotten. Soon less than one-third of the grandchildren of the pioneers could read or write Arabic. By the mid-1920s the most important Arab American newspaper, *Syrian World*, was published in English.

The use of Arabic died out for another reason. After World War I, the United States passed the Immigration Act of 1924, which made it much harder for immigrants to enter the country. Thus those who were already here were not joined by Arabic-speaking newcomers who could have helped them to revive the language. "The immigration quota act limited the entry of Arabic speakers at the same time that the accelerated Americanization process was eroding the use of Arabic,"[21] writes Alixa Naff.

As the use of Arabic died out, and memories of their homelands grew dim, the Syrian pioneers could certainly claim that they had accomplished what they had set out to do: They had become Americans.

CHAPTER THREE

Turmoil in the Middle East: The Second Wave

The Syrian pioneers secured a foothold in America that laid the basis for Arab American life. Few Arabs followed their path to America in the period between the two world wars, however. Only after the end of World War II did a substantial number of Arabs begin to immigrate to America once again. The vast majority of these immigrants arrived after the Immigration Act of 1965 reopened America's doors to worldwide immigration. Between 1965 and 1992, roughly four hundred thousand Arabs immigrated to America. This second wave of Arab immigration included many well-educated profession-als, and a majority of them were Muslim (60 percent).

The second wave immigrants arrived from a variety of new countries that were created after the end of World War I. These new nations were carved from the defeated Ottoman Empire by the victori-ous European powers, without regard to the interests of the Arab inhabitants. At first Britain and France kept control over these Arab lands under temporary gov-ernments called mandates, but gradually they granted their mandates indepen-dence. In the years following World War II, immigrants from Arab lands could thus identify themselves by their nationalities;

they were now known as Lebanese, Jordanians, and Iraqis, for example.

Increasingly, however, Arabs saw themselves as one people. Although Arab nations were now independent, their resentment toward Europe from the mandate era and beyond still existed. Out of this resentment and a desire for Arab pride, an ideology called Pan-Arabism was born. This emphasized a universal Arab identity over any national one. Thus immigrants from the Arab world increasingly identified themselves as Arab, regardless of their nationality or religion.

A New Kind of Immigrant: The Refugee

Arabs emigrated from many countries in the second wave, but some researchers estimate that more Palestinians left than any other group. The Palestinians arrived in

---

An Egyptian Explains Her Desire to Emigrate

Many second wave immigrants came to America to study or to teach at American universities. Egyptian-born Leila Ahmed went first to England to earn her doctorate before coming to America, where she currently teaches at Harvard University. In her autobiography A Border Passage: From Cairo to America—a Woman's Journey, *Ahmed discusses the many frustrations her family experienced living in Egypt under President Gamal Nasser. Her father opposed many of Nasser's policies and as a result, her family was harassed by the government. Egyptian officials made it difficult for Ahmed to obtain a passport to resume her studies in England, but she persisted:*

I've never been sure why I could not take no for an answer. Being compelled to stay in Egypt, being compelled to give up my studies [in England], felt to me like a sentence of doom. There's no doubt that my family's difficulties in Nasser's Egypt, and the bleakness of the future I myself now faced there, were key in my determination to get out, as were my hopes and ambitions for professional and intellectual development. But it was more than that. I needed to understand myself and I believed that the path to understanding lay in returning to England and to graduate studies there. I believed, moreover, that I would not find that same understanding in a university in Egypt.

There was something else, too, a shadow always there, adding to my sense of desperate resolve. My aunt Aida had committed suicide a few months after I had come home [from England] to Egypt. I had grieved at her death, and now her despair became hauntingly real to me. I feared that a despair like that might overtake me if I found myself trapped in Egypt forever, unable to go on with my life.

America as refugees. A refugee is some-one who is forced to flee his or her home-land, and who upon returning would face grave danger.

Palestine remained a mandate under the control of the British until 1947, when the United Nations divided it in two—one homeland for the Jews and another for the Palestinians. The Palestinians became refugees when, on the eve of Israeli inde-pendence, war broke out and five Arab states attacked Israel in 1948. Most of the Arab population that lived within Israel's borders (which had expanded by the end of the war) fled their homelands and sought refuge elsewhere. Historian Don Peretz writes,

> Fear gave way to panic, and by the end of May, most Arab villagers and townsmen had fled to the neighbor-ing Arab countries. As the conflict steadily grew more desperate, thou-sands of Arabs, then hundreds of thousands, fled for safety, so that by the end of the fighting, early in 1949, there were nearly 750,000 Palestine Arab refugees in Lebanon, Syria, Jordan, and the Egyptian-occupied Gaza strip in southern Palestine.[22]

The flight of the Palestinians was very hasty. Without warning a village might come under attack from Israelis, usually at night. In the ensuing panic, family members might get separated. Disorga-nized and lacking up-to-date weapons to fight, many Palestinians fled. Most be-lieved they were leaving their homes only temporarily, until the fighting ended.

Sometimes a family would ask a neighbor to watch over their home, furnishings, and farmland, only to discover that the neigh-bor himself had fled as well. After the fighting ended, many Palestinians tried to return to their homes. Israel had won the war, however, and refused to let the vast majority of these Palestinians return. In the process they lost their land, busi-nesses, and homes.

Life as a Refugee

In neighboring countries, most Palestini-ans lived in refugee camps administered by the United Nations. Israel granted cit-izenship to Palestinians already within its borders and expected that nearby Arab na-tions would do the same; in fact at the time only Jordan gave Palestinians citi-zenship rights. For this reason, many Palestinian refugees entered the United States as citizens of Jordan or as arrivals from Egypt, Syria, and other nearby coun-tries. This makes it hard for historians to know the exact numbers of Palestinian im-migrants to arrive in America.

For those Palestinians with little or no education, economic prospects were very bleak. The host countries like Jordan and Syria were often poor themselves. Most Palestinians were forced to work as day laborers in agriculture or construction work, at meager wages with no job secu-rity. Some could find no work at all. They also had to endure the shame of being out-casts in a country not their own.

Some Palestinians chose to give up their official status as refugees and live outside the refugee camps in other Arab countries, although in doing so they gave up their rights to aid from the United Nations and the hoped-for right to return to their lands. Others remained in refugee camps where they tried to further their education, which the Palestinians viewed as the most effective means toward a better life.

The Palestinians tried to reconstruct their old kinship networks in the refugee camps as best they could, naming their new residences after the villages they had left behind, for example. The first generation of exiles passed on to future generations of Palestinians this persistent longing for the homelands, even though their children and grandchildren had grown up elsewhere. The Palestinians who sought refuge in America brought with them this longing to return as well.

During the Six-Day War of 1967, Israel was once again victorious against the combined effort of several Arab countries. Afterward, Israel occupied more of the remaining territory set aside for a Palestinian state, including the West Bank of the Jordan River, the Gaza Strip, and the Palestinian sector of Jerusalem. The Six-Day War initiated the greatest wave of Palestinian immigration to America, mainly from the cities of Jerusalem, Ra-

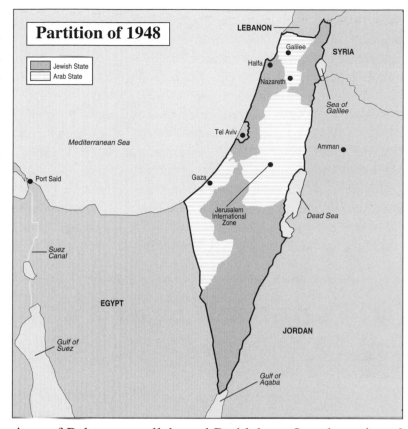

Partition of 1948

Jewish State
Arab State

LEBANON
Galilee
SYRIA
Halfa
Nazareth
Sea of Galilee
Mediterranean Sea
Tel Aviv
Amman
Port Said
Gaza
Jerusalem International Zone
Dead Sea
Suez Canal
EGYPT
JORDAN
Gulf of Suez
Gulf of Aqaba

mallah, and Bethlehem. Israel continued to build Jewish settlements in these areas and, according to Louise Cainkar, the "Israeli concentration on land confiscation in these areas in the 1970's and 1980's created an even greater emigrant push." [23] From 1965 to 1992, it is estimated that sixty-five thousand Palestinians carrying Jordanian passports entered the United States.

The First to Leave

The first Palestinians to immigrate to America after the creation of Israel were those who already had relatives living in America. There were, in fact, quite a few Palestinians already settled in the United States by that time; approximately 10 percent of the Syrian immigrants who arrived in America before 1924 came from Palestine, then part of Greater Syria. These first wave relatives had most likely sent money and other help back to their relatives in Palestine. With this added income, many Palestinians had left farming behind and become businesspeople, teachers, or other professionals. These groups had the wherewithal and know-how to leave first.

Their routes to America were various. Some well-educated Palestinians who were in America to study found unexpectedly that they could never return to their homeland. This is what happened to Princeton professor Hisham Sharabi, who left war-torn Palestine in 1947 to study at the University of Chicago. In his autobiography he recounted what it felt like to be in America at this time:

> Here I was in America at last. My dreams had come true. I had arrived at the University of Chicago, and now I was in my private room at the

The Creation of Israel

Events following the creation of Israel in 1948 caused thousands of Arab refugees to flee their homelands for America. During World War I, when the debate over statehood began, the British issued the Balfour Declaration, which stated that the British favored the establishment of a national home for the Jewish people in Palestine, provided this did not infringe on the rights of the Arab population. While some Jews had lived in Palestine for centuries, and many immigrated there throughout the nineteenth and early twentieth centuries, Arabs formed the majority.

In 1947 the United Nations decided to divide Palestine into two states: one for the Jews and another for the Arabs. Thirty-three countries, a majority of the United Nations General Assembly, voted to approve this plan. The Arabs, however, were opposed to the division of Palestine, and no Arab country voted for the plan.

As the British withdrew from Palestine in 1948 and Israel declared itself a nation, war broke out between the Arabs and Israelis. Five Arab nations attacked Israel, but Israel successfully fought back. By the end of the war, Israel had expanded her borders to include approximately one-third to one-half of the land that the United Nations had reserved for the Arab state of Palestine. The remaining land of Palestine was taken by Jordan (the West Bank of the Jordan River) or by Egypt (the Gaza Strip).

Although Arabs living within the original borders of Israel were permitted to live in Israel as citizens, most of them fled the horrors of war. As a result, almost two-thirds of the Palestinian population, approximately 750,000 people, became refugees.

International House. But a feeling of loneliness suddenly overtook me. My heart was about to burst, and my eyes filled with tears. I wanted to go home. I wanted to return to my homeland. . . . I never thought I would spend most of my life in America, and that when I did return to my homeland it would be for only a short and tragic period.[24]

Many other Palestinians came to America after living in refugee camps in Jordan, Lebanon, and Syria. Some Palestinians reestablished their lives in other Arab countries such as Egypt or Iraq, and later decided that coming to America would offer them better prospects in life. In his autobiography, *Out of Place*, Professor Edward Said of Columbia University remembers life in Egypt after many of his family members had fled there from Palestine: "What overcomes me now is the scale of dislocation our family and friends experienced. . . . As a boy of twelve and a half in Cairo, I often saw the sadness and destitution in the faces and lives of people I had formerly known as ordinary middle-class people in Palestine. . . . All of us seemed to have given up on Palestine as a place, never to be returned to, barely mentioned, missed silently and pathetically."[25] From Egypt Edward Said came to America to study, and then remained there.

Palestinian American Shaw Dalall, who is now a professor at Cornell University, also remained elsewhere in the Middle East before immigrating to America. In an interview he recounted,

After the war of 1947–48 in Palestine, my family was so worried. I was the youngest of eight children, and my family was worried about me staying there [in Palestine], so they sent me to Kuwait. I stayed there with my first cousin for 45 days. Then he found me a job at the age of 15 at a hospital, which was run by American missionaries. I met an American priest. . . . He helped me to apply to about 25 colleges. . . . Cornell University [in upstate New York] . . . offered me a free tuition scholarship, and I came to the States with about $27.00 in my pocket.[26]

The Palestinians who fared best in America arrived with excellent credentials or earned them soon after, like professors Said and Dalall. Palestinians who had family members already in America were likely to thrive as well. Louise Cainkar, who has studied Palestinian immigrants, writes,

Family members . . . received rapid economic benefit from the resources, business experience, and networks their predecessors had established. Newcomers in these family chains did not have to endure the struggle to gain solid economic footing in the United States like the initial early immigrants. Whether they came before or after 1967, relatives of the early immigrants moved quickly, economically speaking, into middle-class U.S. society.[27]

This group of Arab refugees was forced to live in tents after Israeli forces demolished their homes. The Six-Day War of 1967 left many Arab families homeless.

Subsequent waves of Palestinians, those with poor educational backgrounds and no prior family connections in America, have had a more difficult time making it in America.

The Arab Brain Drain and the Immigration Act of 1965

One thing that fostered a surge of Arab immigration to America was the passage of the Immigration and Nationality Act of 1965. It was passed just before the Six-Day War of 1967 after which many Arabs, including the Palestinians, immigrated to America. This law overturned the restrictive quota-based Immigration Act of 1924 and enabled twenty thousand immigrants to enter the United States from every country each year, favoring those with occupational skills and higher education.

Many educated Arabs throughout the Arab world were poised to take advantage of the act. In between the two world wars, when Europeans controlled most of the Middle East, Arabs had profited from the many schools set up by the English and French. After Arab countries became independent nations, many established their own universities, especially Egypt, Syria, Lebanon, and Iraq. These schools produced an educated Arab elite consisting of doctors, teachers, engineers, and scientists who were welcomed by the U.S.

Greater Israel
AFTER JUNE 20, 1967

Israeli territory
1949–June 10, 1967

Israeli conquests
June 5–11, 1967

LEBANON

Mediterranean Sea

Haifa

Sea of Galilee

GOLAN HEIGHTS

Nazareth

Tel Aviv-Jaffa

WEST BANK

Jordan River

Ashdod

Ashkelon

Gaza

Jericho

Gaza Strip

Jerusalem

Amman

Hebron

Dead Sea

NEGEV DESERT

SINAI PENINSULA

EGYPT

JORDAN

Gulf of Suez

Elat

Gulf of Aqaba

Strait of Tiran

SAUDI ARABIA

immigration service because they would enrich America with their skills. In the second wave of Arab immigration, women came in numbers almost equal to men. Like their male counterparts, an increasing number of Arab women arrived in America as professionals.

Thousands of these Arabs left a variety of countries to take advantage of this new policy, especially between 1968 and 1971. A Lebanese immigrant in America, Dr. Tony Khater, explained in an interview, "Lebanon is one of the most densely populated countries in the world. University graduates were on the increase there in the late 1960's and early 1970's, and they had no job prospects. Hence they turned to the United States."[28] During those years Egypt alone lost seven thousand professionally trained emigrants.

As good as the universities in the Middle East might be, they could not compare to the top schools in the United States, especially in medicine and the sciences. U.S. universities were well endowed with money and well equipped with the latest technologies in scientific research. They attracted some of the best scientists and thinkers from around the world, thus providing an unparalleled community of researchers with whom to work. Some Arabs came to America to further their academic careers and credentials and then returned home to the Middle East, bringing their newly acquired expertise with them. Many could not resist remaining in America permanently because they could acquire more money, a more comfortable lifestyle, and better professional contacts.

Disillusionment with Arab Governments

Another reason why Arabs left their homelands during the second wave was that many became disillusioned with their governments. This disillusionment slowly developed over the latter half of the twentieth century; however, in the 1950s many Arabs had high hopes for their countries. Some nations, like Iraq, were rich with oil resources and modernizing rapidly. Others were inspired by the vision of Pan Arabism laid out by Egyptian president Gamal Nasser. As hopes for a brighter future in these countries began to fade, however, many Arabs thought of leaving.

In Egypt, for example, the 1967 and 1973 wars with Israel were a substantial drain on the economy and delayed hoped-for prosperity. They also demoralized the population as the defeats humiliated Egypt and other Arab nations who lost to the much smaller, but better equipped, Israeli army. Still more young men left the country to avoid the draft. Egyptians thus came to America in significant numbers after both of those wars; by 1979 forty-four thousand had settled in America, including Egyptian Copts (a Christian sect), Protestants, and Muslims.

Other Egyptians left as they saw their society slide into mismanagement. A rapid rise in the population of Egypt, coupled with poor governmental planning, created a deeper divide between the rich and the poor. In 1977 mass riots broke out, as demonstrators protested rising inflation and food prices. When criticized, the government responded by cracking down on dissidents, limiting freedom of the press, and jailing people holding unpopular political views. Well-educated and ambitious Egyptians grew frustrated with their society and its all-too-slow march toward democracy, prompting many to seek better economic opportunities in America. Like so many Arabs who arrived in America before them, the Egyptians settled in major U.S. cities where they have prospered.

Similar disillusionment developed in Iraq. Iraqis came to America in small numbers in the early years of Arab immigration, but in significant numbers since then. Between 1967 and 1988, for example, more than forty thousand Iraqis settled in the United States. Most left to flee Saddam Hussein's rule, which brutalized the country. His reign of terror began in 1979 when he usurped power by ruthlessly

Edward Said, American Spokesperson for the Palestinian Cause

Edward W. Said, the acclaimed professor at Columbia University, was America's foremost spokesperson for the Palestinian cause. Said was born in 1935 in Palestine and grew up in Jerusalem and in Cairo, Egypt. Like so many of the second wave immigrants, his family was well-educated, well-connected, and well-to-do. Said's father, who like his mother was a Christian, ran the Cairo branch of the family's business, the Standard Stationery Company. It became the foremost office equipment company in the Middle East. Said's father, with the help of his wife, was the first person to design an Arabic-letter typewriter for the Royal Typewriter Company. Edward's many aunts, uncles, and cousins lived in Jerusalem, where Edward spent much of his time among his extended family. He was educated in elite English and American schools in Cairo and Palestine.

When Said was twelve years old, the United Nations divided Palestine into Jewish and Arab halves. It was hard for him to understand what was happening to his homeland, and his family avoided discussing politics. Still, he could sense his family's sorrow as Palestine was partitioned into various zones.

As war broke out in Palestine in 1948, Said and his family left Jerusalem immediately for their home in Cairo, Egypt. There they were joined by more family members who were forced to flee Palestine. Said's father had gained U.S. citizenship as a first wave immigrant, but had later returned to the Middle East to raise a family. Because his father was already a U.S. citizen, Edward immigrated to America where he went to boarding school and then to Princeton and Harvard universities for his education. He went on to become a world-renowned scholar, author, and spokesperson for the Palestinian people. He died in 2003.

murdering his political opponents. More misery befell Iraqis in 1980 when Saddam Hussein proclaimed war against Iraq's powerful neighbor, Iran. The war dragged on for eight long years, finally ending in a standoff in 1988. It cost Iraq a million battlefield casualties and racked up a huge debt of $60 billion. Young Iraqi men emigrated if they could to escape the draft, while others sought better economic opportunities in America.

The desire for political freedom was, perhaps, the most important reason why many Iraqis left their country. Karim Alkadhi, who brought his family to America in 1980, explained, "I didn't come to the United States for the dollars that grew on trees. . . . What counts is that [in America] I can criticize anyone without endangering my life or my freedom."[29] The 1991 Persian Gulf War spawned even more immigration; overall it is estimated that fifty thousand Iraqis, belonging to a variety of religious groups, have left Iraq and settled in the United States since 1991. According to the *New York Times*, "Many fled under conditions of extreme duress, and most can list a relative who has been killed or imprisoned by Saddam Hussein's regime."[30]

A story that is typical of poorer Iraqi immigrants is that of Haeder Mouhammed, age thirty-two. Mouhammed is the transportation coordinator for an Islamic school in New York. One of his brothers was shot in the Iran-Iraq War, a second was imprisoned, and the third was killed for deserting the army. After seeing what happened to his brothers, Mouhammed did all he could to escape from military duty. He hid on the outskirts of Baghdad and slowly made his way toward the Syrian border. He worked at a variety of low-paying jobs in Damascus, Syria, before he came to New York, knowing just six words of English.

These Arab students learn an Arabic grammar lesson. Many well-educated Arabs have immigrated to America seeking a better life.

Escaping Civil War

Also contributing to the second wave of Arab immigration was the onset of civil war in several Middle Eastern nations. Such countries were torn apart by fighting, which devastated their populations and prompted more immigrants to leave their homes for America. Lebanon was one such nation with an exceptionally brutal civil war. Over fifty thousand Lebanese have immigrated since 1967. Many of them left Lebanon beginning in 1975 when fighting broke out.

The origins of the Lebanese civil war go back to the delicate balance between its Christian and Muslim populations. After the Arab-Israeli wars, Lebanon took in three hundred thousand Palestinian refugees who were mainly Muslims. After many years of living in abysmal conditions in refugee camps, the Palestinians organized commando groups to attack Israel. This created a crisis for Lebanon, with Muslims mainly supporting the Palestinian attacks and Christians not. Eventually the factions within Lebanon went to war against each other.

The Lebanese civil war flared on and off for fifteen years. In the process it destroyed Beirut, one of the great cities of the Middle East. As a consequence of the war, casualties mounted to a quarter of a million. Almost a third of the country's population of 3.3 million people became homeless. The country was devastated economically: 35 percent of its factories were destroyed. With such devastation it is not surprising, then, that between 1965 and 1992 roughly ninety thousand Lebanese (including some Palestinians arriving from Lebanon) came to the United States. Many Lebanese joined families in America who had immigrated there earlier.

Similarly, many Yemenis left their home in Yemen to flee a civil war that broke out in the 1960s when revolutionaries tried to overthrow the monarchy. For many years the country was divided into two warring halves; only in 1990 did the two Yemens successfully reunite. In addition to turmoil brought about by war, economic prospects in Yemen were bleak, with at times more than a third of the population unemployed. The search for employment brought many Yemenis to America, up to ten thousand between 1965 and 1992.

Arab Identity in America

The second wave of Arab immigrants thus included Palestinians, Jordanians, Egyptians, Iraqis, Lebanese, Syrians, and Yemenis. They brought an array of religious practices with them to America. Arab Muslims were inspired by the fact that relatives and friends had prospered here while being guaranteed the same freedom of worship promised to all Americans. Significant numbers of Christians came as well, like the Iraqi Chaldeans and Egyptian Copts.

Despite their diversity, the second wave Arabs arrived in America with a strong sense that they shared an overriding identity: they were Arabs. The idea of Pan Arabism, that is, the existence of a cultural connection between all Arabs no matter what their national origins, had been fostered across the Arab world by Gamal Nasser, Egypt's president in the 1950s and 1960s. Nasser spearheaded the Pan-Arabic movement during the Cold War as a way for Arab nations to stand independent of both the United States and its allies, and the Soviet Communist bloc. Second wave Arab immigrants arrived in America with a sense of belonging to this wide community with international dimensions.

The second wave of newcomers arrived in America at an opportune time to foster pride in being both Arab and American. In the 1960s and 1970s Americans were encouraged to celebrate their ethnic roots and be proud of their differences. This was quite different from the goal of the first wave: that ethnic groups disappear into the melting pot of America where they would meld to become more alike. The very term "Arab American" was a product of this period, where remaining Arab was just as important to immigrants as becoming American.

One key to igniting a sense of Arab American identity was the revitalization of the Arabic language. While the offspring of the first wave immigrants could no longer speak Arabic, second wave immigrants speaking it arrived in force. According to historian Alixa Naff, one result is that in recent times "Syrian-Americans are showing an interest in their ethnicity, learning about their cultures, and taking at least some colloquial Arabic at college or doing research on Arabs and Arab-Americans in graduate school."[31]

The second wave also brought a new concern for the plight of Arabs in the Middle East, especially the Palestinian refugees. The Six-Day War traumatized the entire Arab American community, who felt that the American news media presented slanted accounts of the war that favored the Israeli side. "The war itself also produced soul-searching on the part of many Arab Americans, old and new, and often reinforced or strengthened their Arab identity,"[32] writes political scientist Michael Suleiman.

The first organization to use "Arab American" in its title was the Association of Arab-American University Graduates. It was founded in 1967 by Arab American professors and their graduate students with doctors, lawyers, and other professionals. Their initial goal was to form a group that could effectively voice opposition to America's overwhelming support for Israel after the Six-Day War. They went on to foster academic research about the Arab American community and publish many scholarly articles and books. Thus, out of the crucible of loss and pain over events in the Middle East, the first wave immigrants and their offspring and the newly arrived second wave immigrants began to forge one identity: the Arab Americans.

CHAPTER FOUR

Old Roots, New Branches: Arab Religions in America

From New York to San Francisco and from Dallas to Detroit, Arab Americans put down roots across America. Wherever they settled, they faced the perennial issue confronting all immigrant groups: how to maintain their traditions while assimilating into the American mainstream. While certain cultural practices of their homelands were relatively easy for Arabs to transplant in America, such as their foods, festivals, and music, the immigrants found it more difficult to maintain their religious traditions. This is because Arab immigrants brought with them a variety of religious practices with which Americans were unfamiliar. In most cases the Arab immigrants did not have the option of joining preexisting congregations, they had to establish their own churches and mosques. Doing so took time, money, determination, and the ability to withstand pressures to conform to American religious practices.

Arab Christians in America

A few Arabs arrived in America as Protestants, converted in their homelands by Protestant missionaries. But the majority of the Arab Christian immigrants practiced forms of Eastern Christianity; these included the Syrian Orthodox, Melchite,

During a visit to America, Shedouh III, head of the Egyptian Coptic Church, blesses Arab children. Most Arab American Christians practice forms of Eastern Christianity.

Maronite, Egyptian Coptic, and Iraqi Chaldean sects. Their beliefs set them apart from other Americans who were unfamiliar with these traditions.

Eastern churches differed from Roman Catholicism in a number of significant ways, like saying mass in a variety of languages and not acknowledging the supremacy of the pope in Rome. Eastern Christian traditions also do not require their priests to be celibate as in the Roman Catholic tradition. A variety of arguments over church doctrine further divided Eastern Christian sects from Western Catholicism.

Unfamiliar with Eastern churches, many Americans assumed that they were backward or inferior to Western traditions. Sociologist Philip M. Kayal writes, "East-ern rites were looked down upon socially, being associated with peasant culture, whereas Latin rite [Roman Catholicism] stood for European and Christian civilization, progress, prestige, education and commerce."[33] In America, practitioners of Eastern faiths therefore came under pressure to convert or modify their traditions if they wanted to move up the social ladder in America.

Preserving the Faith

The first goal of the immigrants was to build their own churches. Until they could afford to build, they met in homes of the immigrants or bought churches of other faiths and transformed them. Between 1890 and 1895 one Melchite, one Maronite, and one Syrian Orthodox church were built in New York City. Seventy-five Eastern rite churches were established throughout twenty-eight states by the 1920s.

Each church became the focal point of many community activities. Weddings were the grand events that brought whole communities together in celebration. Mary Macron remembers an Eastern rite wedding in Cleveland this way:

With their husbands and children [the women] would form an entourage to the bride's house to bring her to the church. . . . The rings were blessed with much chanting, and crowns were placed upon the heads of bride and groom—blessed and inter-changed three times—as the cantor sang and the priest prayed over them. The priest would then lead the couple around the altar and along the aisles of the church, all the while chanting the nuptial liturgy and swinging the thurible [incense burner] vigorously as the sweet and heavy vapors of incense filled the air.[34]

As ceremonies like these were recreated in America, Eastern Christian immigrants took comfort in the old, familiar ways of their homelands, over eight thousand miles away.

Making Adjustments

Gradually the Eastern faiths changed to accommodate to life in America, some more than others. The American-born offspring of the Syrian Orthodox could no longer understand the languages of their parents and grandparents, and so the liturgy was translated into English. Men and women, separated in church in their homelands, stood side by side in America. The Syrian Orthodox calendar was also adjusted so that religious festivals would coincide with Western Christian traditions.

While these were significant changes, the Syrian Orthodox held their ground better against changing their traditions than did the Maronites and Melchites, for example. Centuries ago both of these faiths moved closer to the Roman Catholic tradition than did the Syrian Orthodox. When Maronite and Melchite immigrants arrived in America, they felt comfortable worshipping in Roman Catholic churches. Even when they established their own churches, the Maronites and Melchites tended to Latinize their rituals, bringing them closer to the Roman Catholicism practiced by other Americans. Maronite priests adopted the Roman tradition of remaining celibate. Adjustments such as these gave the Maronites greater social status in America, but not necessarily with other Arab Christian groups.

As they drew closer to the church of Rome, Arab American Melchites and Maronites were deemed to be more acceptable marriage partners for Roman Catholics from other ethnic backgrounds, such as the Italians or Irish. Intermarriage helped their communities to move into the American mainstream, but it also

The Mosque in America

The most recognizable architectural features of a mosque are its dome and minaret. From inside a mosque the dome creates a heavenly space. The use of a tall minaret developed because it enabled the muezzin's voice to be heard more widely as he called the faithful to prayer. Both minaret and dome give the mosque its distinct silhouette, which worshippers can see far on the horizon. Many mosques in America have neither of these two features, however. Of the more than one thousand mosques in America, only about one hundred were built as such. Most mosques are former churches, community centers, or even stores.

Mosques have other features, such as fountains so that worshippers can ritually cleanse themselves before prayer. Mosques also have rugs on which worshippers kneel to pray, and a *quiblah*, which faces in the direction of Mecca. Worshippers pray facing the *quiblah* wall, which is marked by a mihrab, a niche that is often beautifully decorated with geometric designs and verses of the Koran in Arabic.

The most prominent mosque in America is the Islamic Center of Washington, D.C., built in 1957, which is now protected as a historical building. It has elements of Egyptian and Turkish architecture. One of the most striking mosques in America is Dar al Islam built in Abiquiu, New Mexico, in 1981. Its Egyptian architecture blends traditional Islamic forms with features of Southwest adobe architecture. The Islamic Cultural Center of New York City was erected in 1991. It was designed by an American architectural firm with the help of funds from Kuwait and Saudi Arabia. Although it has a striking minaret, the call to prayer is made within the mosque only, not to the surrounding neighborhood as it would be in the Middle East. Mosques have adapted to the American landscape, and in turn the American landscape has been transformed by them.

threatened their separate identities. Despite their many accommodations to Roman Catholicism, Melchites and Maronites have still maintained distinct traditions, and in recent years have reclaimed some of their original practices.

Other Arab Christian denominations have successfully established themselves in America more recently, such as the Egyptian Coptic and Iraqi Chaldean. Although Arab Christians have tailored their religious practices to suit life in America, they have succeeded in transplanting many denominations, thereby adding to the diversity of Christian worship in America.

Building Mosques

Muslim Arab immigrants changed America's religious landscape even more dramatically by bringing with them the practice of Islam, today the world's second largest religion. When Muslim Arabs first arrived in America, there were no mosques. This was not an impediment to transporting their religion, however, because Muslims are not required to pray in a mosque. A prayer rug pointing toward Mecca, an empty space free of the distractions of everyday life, and water with which to cleanse oneself before prayer are all that is needed to create a ritually clean space for worship.

At first Arab Muslims said daily prayers in their homes and, when permitted, their work spaces. A mosque was needed, however, to bring the Muslim community, or *ummah*, together, an important function of the mosque in Islam. Once Arab Muslims knew they were in America to stay, they pooled their efforts to raise funds to build them. The first

mosques were dedicated in Michigan, Indiana, North Dakota, and Iowa, beginning in the 1920s. While some mosques were built as such, many more were once stores, churches, and empty buildings that were transformed into mosques.

Muslim Worship in America

The first generation of Muslim Arabs made many adjustments to life in America, as did their Arab Christian counterparts. Several changes were made regarding daily prayers. Devout Muslims are expected to pray five times a day. Prayer need not be performed in a mosque except on Friday, the holiest day of the week for Muslims. This is when Muslims (primarily the men) are expected to attend noontime prayers at the mosque and hear the weekly sermon. In America, however,

When he is unable to pray in a mosque, this American Muslim boy, like most American Muslims, practices his faith in his home.

working men found it very difficult to leave their jobs to pray at the mosque on Fridays.

This conflict led many Muslims to adopt Sunday, the Christian day of worship, as their time for communal worship and for Sunday school. The mosque itself took on many roles in the community it did not have in the homelands, such as a place for large group dinners, bake sales, and bazaars. These functions served the social, rather than religious, needs of the immigrants who wanted a place to nurture their ties to one another and to their homelands in a shared space. According to a group of researchers, "Funerals, weddings, holidays, and celebrations were constantly attended in the mosque, so much so that the ground floor, the 'social domain' of the mosque, saw greater use over the years than the upper floor or 'sanctuary' [where prayers are performed]."[35]

In America the roles of both worshippers and spiritual leaders adapted to meet new needs. Women took on more prominent roles in mosques than they did in their homelands. Women served as fundraisers for the building of mosques, organizers of celebrations, and teachers in religious schools. In America the role of the imam, or spiritual leader, changed too. Imams in the homeland served to interpret Islamic law as it relates to daily life. This might involve ensuring that Islamic practices were followed concerning divorce, property rights, and the investment of money. In America, however, the imam became a general counselor and family guide, taking on a role more similar to

that of a minister. In a new land unfamiliar with Islam, the imam also took on the role of explaining Islam to Americans of other faiths at interfaith gatherings or at schools, for example.

A New Infusion of Religious Practice

Recent Muslim Arab immigrants have encouraged stricter adherence to what they deem is traditional Islam. As a result, a growing number of Arab Americans are choosing to send their children to *madrassas*, Muslim religious schools, instead of public schools so that they can integrate the practice of Islam into their daily lives more effectively. Another recent change is that American mosques today are importing imams trained in leading Islamic centers from the Arab homelands. This has caused tension in some communities between Muslim Arabs who grew up in America and the newcomers. Author Yvonne Haddad reports, "In an increasing number of Arab Muslim mosques where traditional imams have been installed, women have seen their participation in mosque functions reduced and restricted."[36] This has saddened and angered some Arab American Muslims.

Another change is the revival of *hijab*, the traditional head scarf worn by many Muslim women. While many Muslim Arab American women do not wear a head scarf, a younger generation of women is eager to dress in *hijab*, whether they were born in America or abroad. One Arab Muslim woman who wears *hijab* reported in an interview, "I feel proud be-

American Muslims pray during an Eid al-Fitr ceremony at their mosque. Eid al-Fitr marks the end of the monthlong fast of Ramadan.

cause I like the way I look, the way I look in this society, it makes me show as having a different identity, and I am proud of it."[37] A Muslim father took a different view of *hijab:* "I feel that my wife or daughter if they go shopping in *hijab,* they'll attract more attention [than is proper]. . . . But modest dress (not a miniskirt) is a must."[38]

Rather than accommodating to American ways, Muslim Arab American university students are demanding that U.S. colleges make accommodations for them. Some universities are complying with requests from Muslim students that they be provided with spaces in which to pray five times a day, and food that is *halal*, or ritually clean. Dartmouth is one example of a college that has met these needs. Be-

cause Muslim college students have more than doubled in the past ten years, twenty-seven American colleges have responded by employing imams.

Muslim Holidays Come to America

Muslim Arabs brought with them two important religious holidays, which are now celebrated in America. They are Eid al-Fitr, which concludes the monthlong fast of Ramadan, and Eid al-Adha, celebrated by Muslims worldwide at the end of the hajj, the annual pilgrimage to Mecca. Sometimes Muslims who are not observant throughout the year but who do celebrate these home-based festivities are referred to as "Eid Muslims." Muslims believe that it was during the month of Ramadan that Muhammad received the first verses of the Koran from God. During Ramadan, Islam enjoins all Muslims who are in good health to refrain from eating, drinking, and sexual activity from dawn to sunset. Ramadan is thus a time of reflection, gratitude to God, and remembrance of the needs of the hungry.

Throughout the month, families in America, as elsewhere in the world, come together in the evening to break the fast and eat special foods and sweets. Eid al-Fitr is a very joyous occasion when ex-tended family members come from far and wide to be together for three days to feast and celebrate. Similar festivities mark Eid al-Adha.

Because there are now estimated to be 6 million American Muslims from many different ethnic backgrounds, Ramadan brings Muslim Arab Americans into a wider community of the faithful in America. Despite the strength and comfort gathered from this, especially during the fast, it is much harder to be a Muslim in a non-Muslim country during Ramadan when the rest of the population is eating away.

A Muslim family gathers to break the Ramadan fast. Throughout the month of Ramadan Muslims refrain from eating, drinking, and sexual activity from dawn to sunset.

American schools have become more sensitive to the needs of Muslim students during Ramadan, by not insisting students go to the cafeteria at lunchtime, for example, and by sometimes setting aside a special study hall where observant students may go instead.

Sometimes Muslims find special ways to stay connected with their non-Muslim friends even when they cannot eat with them throughout the day. One college student remembers,

> We Muslim students sometimes organized pre-dawn trips to the International House of Pancakes [so that we could eat before sunrise when the fast begins]. We would all pile in the school van at around 3:00 a.m., arguing . . . over the best route to take. . . . One time, I brought my non Muslim friends along. . . . But we were not just [divided into] "the Muslim girls" and "the [other] friends . . . "; we were more than the sum of our parts. We were all observing Ramadan.[39]

Because Muslims use a lunar calendar, the eids fall on different days of the year over the course of many years. In 1997 Christmas fell during the month of Ramadan. The coinciding of the holidays was both positive and negative, as one *New York Times* reporter noted: "On the one hand, it gives practicing American Muslims something to celebrate this year. But the public displays of Christmas trees and [Hanukkah] menorahs . . . also remind them just how marginal Islam . . . still is in the public culture."[40] In 2001 Thanksgiving fell during Ramadan. Many Arab Americans felt this was an appropriate time to celebrate both holidays that give thanks to God, making the fast-breaking evening meal a Thanksgiving one as well.

Different Rates of Assimilation

When Muslim Arab Americans live in large conclaves, isolated from other Americans, they hold on to their own traditions longer, but assimilate less quickly. This is what has happened in the Greater Detroit area, which is estimated to have the largest Arab community in the country, with several hundred thousand residents. Among these are Muslim Yemeni, Palestinian, Iraqi, and Lebanese Arab Americans drawn to the region to work in the auto industry. Muslim residents tend to remain in Dearborn generation after generation. They like living close to the auto factories in which they work, and they take comfort in living among fellow Muslims.

This gives Dearborn, especially its south end, a distinctly Arab Muslim flavor. According to the Abrahams,

> Men and women can often be seen in their dresses of national origin as if they were still in their villages. Groups of men stroll along Dix Avenue and congregate at street corners near coffeehouses, restaurants, billiard halls, and the nearby mosque. The regular calls of the *muezzin* (the prayer caller) at the mosque are now carried across a public address system which can be heard throughout

the area, reminding the Muslim residents of their obligations. As one passes along the commercial district (the *souq* or marketplace as it is sometimes referred to) one engages many of the sights and sounds familiar to the bazaars so common in the countries from which these immigrants came.[41]

Christian Arabs in areas like Greater Detroit have assimilated more rapidly because they are more widely dispersed. They tend to move up and out of the inner city in pursuit of various occupations and the "American dream"—a house in the suburbs. There they live among Americans of many different backgrounds and so assimilate more quickly.

Some Arab immigrants have had a difficult time assimilating because of their political views. Even after years in America, many Palestinians (both Muslims and Christians) still view themselves as refugees who will eventually return home to Palestine. A general sense of frustration has set in due to America's failed efforts to negotiate a lasting peace in the Middle East and to establish a Palestinian state. In addition, most Palestinians continue to believe that America favors Israel in negotiations. This makes many Palestinian Americans feel frustrated and isolated.

According to the *Los Angeles Times*, "Part of the alienation [felt by Palestinian Americans] . . . stems from a conviction that the Palestinian side of the story is rarely heard in the U.S., that there is a double standard about the lives lost to violence." The article goes on to quote Lily Karam, a Palestinian businesswoman, who says, "We came [to America] seeking freedom and dignity. . . . Now I feel so lonely. . . . I love the American people, and suddenly I feel so alienated."[42] Feelings of gratitude toward America, mixed with anger at America's policies in the Middle East, cause Palestinian Americans, as well as other Arab Americans, to hold bittersweet feelings toward the country that has extended them refuge.

Marriage Patterns and Assimilation

Like other customs, Arab marriage patterns also underwent change in America and affected assimilation patterns. In the Middle East, marriages are important not just to the individuals getting married, but to their entire families. For this reason, parents play a decisive role in finding a spouse for their child either by arranging the marriage or by approving of it. In most traditional Arab cultures, the bride leaves her home to become a member of the bridegroom's family. Children are expected to marry within their faith and even within the large extended family—to their cousins, for example.

In America these marriage patterns slowly began to change. For one thing, many states forbade first cousins to marry. Furthermore, in small communities it was not always possible to find a mate of the same nationality and religious background. Thus, if a Syrian Orthodox Catholic could not find another Syrian Orthodox Catholic, he or she might acceptably marry into a Russian or Greek Or-

A traditionally dressed Muslim woman walks along a Detroit street. Many Arab American women enjoy a higher social status and a larger income than they did in their homelands.

thodox family, or even into a Polish or Italian American Catholic family. Families who intermarried in this way tended to Americanize very quickly.

Muslim Arabs also made compromises by marrying Muslims from different countries, or by asking a bride of another faith to convert to Islam. Given the choice of marrying someone of the same nationality but a different religion, or someone of a different nationality of the same religion, people chose to marry within their religions.

Marriage and the Role of Women

As the offspring of Arab immigrants grew up in America, many wanted to adopt American-style dating patterns. In Amer-

ica, individuals are expected to find their own spouses through a series of trial relationships that are initiated on dates or through "hanging out together." Because dating may include sexual activity, and couples in America date even when they do not expect to marry, many traditional Arab parents view dating as a frivolous activity that has the potential of compromising the reputations of their daughters. While sons are allowed some leeway before marriage, daughters of both Christian and Muslim Arab Americans are put under more pressure than their brothers not to date and to marry mates approved, if not directly chosen, by their parents.

The clash of Arab and American social expectations has created conflict within some families, especially those Muslim

Arabic Films and Radio Programs for American Audiences

One way Arabs in America stayed connected to Arabic culture and to each other was by listening to radio broadcasts geared to the Arab American community and by watching films made in the Middle East. In "Cultural Traditions of Early Arab Immigrants to New York," which appears in A Community of Many Worlds: Arab Americans in New York City, *Stanley Rashid recounts how his father went into the business of importing Arabic music and films.*

Arab films first made the scene in New York in 1934. My father, Albert Rashid, presented the first Egyptian films at the Brooklyn Academy of Music every month. His first film was the epic *Ward El Bayda (The White Rose)* starring Mohamed Abdel Wahab. The novelty of seeing a motion picture film in their own language created a stir in the New York Arab community that was unprecedented. The film contained over ten songs. The demand for these songs on records was so great that Rashid began to import records from the Baidaphone Recording Company of Cairo, Egypt.

Albert Rashid's business grew as immigrants in other cities wanted to see these films as well. Soon he was renting the films to Arab American communities as far away as Detroit and Cleveland. Once they had seen the films, Arab Americans around the country wanted to listen to recordings of the music, and so Rashid went into the mail-order business, shipping Arab music across the country.

By the 1940s radio stations catered to the musical tastes of Arab Americans in large cities. Stanley Rashid recalls of these programs that "they hosted a weekly program that ran for nearly twenty years. It served the New York community with local and international news and personals such as marriages and births. It reached nearly every Arab American home in New York."

families who do not believe in dating. Young girls growing up in America today are torn between pleasing their families and adhering to their faith, and enjoying life the American way. They have found some creative solutions to this problem. One is the Muslim prom for girls. It has all the trappings of a regular prom— dressing up, strobe lights, and music—but it is lacking one thing: boys. In this way Muslim girls can have fun while maintaining their own values.

How much Arab women have gained by coming to America depends greatly on their country of origin and social class. To some extent, the Arab women who are most oppressed by policy and custom in their homelands have not been able to come to America at all. For example, in Saudi Arabia women are forbidden to travel without a male escort and may not leave the country without the consent of a male relative. Because only 7 percent of Saudi women work outside the home, few would have the means to emigrate alone even if they were permitted. In countries where there are no such restrictions, custom often prevails. An Egyptian woman recounted,

When I left Egypt in 1976, I knew that I was leaving for good. Because it was very hard for me there. My father could tell me, "Oh, don't do this," and I would stop. I couldn't make a decision about my own life. The fact is I spent a year convincing him to let me come to the States to work on my master's degree. If he had said no at the end, I wouldn't have come, even though I was a grown woman.[43]

A Muslim American of Lebanese descent, Donna Shalala (between former president Clinton and vice president Gore) served as secretary of Health and Human Services under Clinton.

The Coffeehouse: A Place for Men

As Arab men adjusted to life in America, they sought a place of refuge where they could forget about the pressures of learning new ways and find comfort in the old ways they had left behind. Such a place was the local coffeehouse. In Middle Eastern tradition the coffeehouse serves as a meeting place where men drink coffee, talk politics, listen to the radio, and play backgammon, cards, and other games. In America men who might have worked together at the factory during the day gathered at the local coffeehouse at night to share news of their home countries, plan fund-raising events to help the homelands' weather crises, or just enjoy the camaraderie of other Arab Americans.

While coffeehouses were not clubs and there were no official members, outsiders were not welcome. If, for example, a coffeehouse displayed a Lebanese flag on its wall, only Lebanese were welcome. Sometimes each "club" catered to a distinct group from within the homeland, many of whom were related. Here family feuds could be resolved because the owner might indeed be a relative. Often certain tables were by custom reserved for the elders, and no young man would dare to sit at them.

The coffeehouse served the purpose of keeping young men born in America in touch with their Arab roots. While the coffeehouse tradition still survives in America, there are increasingly fewer of them. They thrive only in areas of dense Arab American population, such as Greater Detroit.

On the other hand, some Arab American women resent the stereotype prevalent in America that all Muslim Arab women are oppressed. A Syrian American doctor complained,

I came to this country being an MD [a medical doctor] already. That surprised people. They had the built-in idea that [because] I'm a woman and Arab and Muslim, I shouldn't be a doctor who is outgoing, very independent, and very Westernized. But if you don't look at fanatic groups—fanatic groups in any religion are going to gave you the wrong impression—women are encouraged in Islam, they're encouraged in the Koran [Muslim scripture].[44]

Overall, once in America, Arab women achieve higher status and greater income than they did in their homelands. This gives them greater financial independence in America and therefore more leverage within the family structure than they had in their countries of origin. To fight for the rights of women, some Arab American women have joined feminists in the Arab world as well as feminists from other ethnic backgrounds in America. Part of their goal is to fight stereotypical views of Arab women.

CHAPTER FIVE

Working in America: All Walks of Life

S ince their arrival, Arab Americans have made important contributions to America in all walks of life. While the first wave immigrants were largely illiterate, once in America they put a premium on educating their children. Their offspring, as well as the more recently arrived second wave immigrants who followed in their wake, are doctors, lawyers, auto plant workers, entertainers, farm laborers, journalists, engineers, teachers, and elected officials, to name a few. The vast majority are white-collar workers —business owners, managers, and administrators. A high proportion hold college degrees. It is not surprising, then, that Arab

Americans have incomes that are overall above the national average.

The Auto Workers and Other Jobs in Heavy Industry

Ever since its founding days, the automobile industry has been dependent on the work of Arab Americans and has enabled them to prosper. By the 1920s, when most American families were starting to buy their first car—the affordable, mass-produced Model T Ford—the industry was booming. No wonder, then, that the Arabs who first found work in the automobile plants stayed on.

Farm Work and Migrant Labor

In their homelands, the early Arab immigrants worked on farms rather than in factories. Although in America the vast majority of Arab Americans became city dwellers, the farming tradition was carried on by some. In upstate New York, for example, a substantial number of Lebanese-owned farms exist. Early migrants to California often farmed as well.

Today, most Arab immigrants remain urbanites, except for many Yemenis who play an important role as migrant farmworkers in California's lush San Joaquin Valley, where they pick grapes for the growing California wine industry. While most Arab immigrants have brought their families with them to America, the majority of Yemenis are men who come to America without their families; thus they do not mind being housed in the communal camps set up by the farm owners. Like other migrant laborers who do not speak English, the Yemenis are often taken advantage of by their employers. To help the Yemenis win fair wages, benefits, and safe working conditions, a variety of Arab American groups have come to their aid to inform them of their rights. When the Yemenis can, they move on to owning small stores in areas surrounding the vineyards.

Newly arrived immigrants were well-equipped to work on the assembly lines, piecing together automobile parts as they came down the conveyor belts: This work required little knowledge of English and few prior skills. While a worker in an auto plant did not have the authority to hire a relative, he could nonetheless help a family member find a job and learn the ropes.

Soon, more and more Arabs gravitated to the Detroit area and its suburbs, especially Dearborn, home of the Ford Motor Company. The auto industry has continued to employ many newly arrived Arab immigrants of the second wave, making Greater Detroit the most heavily populated Arab American region of the country.

In heavy industry, work in smaller cities attracted Arab Americans as well. In New Castle, Pennsylvania, first wave immigrants worked in the tin mill. There they settled close to the plants at which they worked, and near the railroads that transported the tin throughout America. In the 1980s, a majority of the Arab Americans in Allentown, Pennsylvania, worked in mills, such as those run by Bethlehem Steel or Western Electric.

The Scholarly Tradition

The vanguard of Arab immigration has often been the students, both male and female, who arrived to study in American universities. While many came intending to return home after completing their degrees, great numbers of them decided to stay on in America to live permanently, as did Edward Said, the distinguished Columbia professor. This was especially so after the Immigration Act of 1965 gave preference to immigrants with higher degrees.

Arab culture has traditionally valued education. Muslim families make it a priority to educate themselves and their children, and regard it as a religious duty. It is not surprising, then, that Arab Americans are well represented as educators, especially at the university level. Arab university professors, both men and women, tend to specialize in scientific research, engineering, or in studies of the Middle East and Islam.

Lebanese American professor Philip Hitti (1886–1978) of Princeton University was a scholar of Arab civilization who cared passionately about the Arab American community. Regarded as the father of Arab American studies, he was a superb teacher who trained many of the great American scholars of Islam and Arab American studies. Palestinian-born professor Edward Said of Columbia University was also a major intellectual figure of the twentieth century and America's foremost spokesperson for the Palestinian cause. His most famous book, *Orientalism*, was translated into twenty-six languages. In it he explores the ways in which Western scholars have misperceived the Middle East.

Arab Americans are proud that two Arab American scientists have won the Nobel Prize in chemistry. Professor Elias Corey of Harvard University, whose prize was awarded in 1990, is currently making headway in new anticancer drugs; some experts believe there is not a pharmaceutical company in the world that has not made use of his discoveries in their laboratories. Professor Ahmed Zewail of the California Institute of Technology was awarded the 1999 Nobel Prize in chemistry. Zewail was educated in Egypt but came to America to earn his Ph.D. Egypt has issued a stamp in his honor.

Writers

During the first half of the twentieth century, when the first wave was assimilating, there were few Arab American writers who drew on their ethnic heritage as a source of inspiration. One Arab American who was an exception was the author and illustrator Kahlil Gibran, who became an American celebrity in the 1920s. Gibran was a Maronite Catholic who was born in 1883 in Greater Syria. In 1895 he immigrated with his mother and siblings to Boston. There his mother peddled lace fabric until the family opened a dry goods store.

Gibran's book of mystical poetry, *The Prophet*, has been in continuous print since it first appeared in 1923. As an artist he illustrated his own books as well as a variety of classic literature from the Middle East. One source of inspiration for his graphic design work was Arabic calligraphy. Because he drew upon aspects of Arab culture at a time when most Syrian immigrants were heavily Americanizing, he still remains a hero in the Arab American community today.

After World War II the second wave immigrants brought with them Arabic traditions that inspired a new generation of talented writers of Arab descent in America.

Ahmed Zewail celebrates winning the Nobel Prize for chemistry in 1999. Educated in Egypt, Zewail earned a Ph.D. in America.

Chief among these is the revival of a poetic form called the *ghazal*. Some scholars believe that it is the oldest poetic form still in use today. *Ghazals* often express love and longing. While they may seem easy to write at first, the best poets know that it takes years of practice to perfect the form.

There are many authors writing today who are inspired by Arab literary tradition and who draw on their own experiences as Arab Americans in their work. Naomi Shihab Nye is one of the best-known Arab American authors writing today. She is a poet, children's book author, and winner of numerous awards, including the Paterson Poetry Prize and four Pushcart Prizes.

Her poetry focuses on details of everyday life that illuminate larger issues and shared connections across ethnic groups. Nye has written many books for young people, including the novel *Habibi*, which draws on her own experience in Jerusalem where she was a high school student. Still other Arab American authors include Gregory Orfalea, who writes poetry as well as works of nonfiction about Arab Americans. Two Lebanese American writers are Elmaz Abinader, who writes poetry, fiction, and essays, and Etel Adnan, a poet, novelist, and painter. Diana Abu-Jaber is a novelist who lives in the United States and Jordan.

Arab Americans in Office

Arab Americans began to participate in American political life at the local level in small towns across America. Here, in their eagerness to Americanize, the Syrians joined the local Rotary and Kiwanis clubs. As prosperous and hardworking members of their towns, Syrians were elected council members, mayors, and even state legislators. It took more time for Arab Americans to make an impact on the national level.

One person who did move into national politics was Philip C. Habib, who became one of America's premier diplomats. He was born in 1920 in Brooklyn, the son of a Lebanese grocer. He eventually became a diplomat serving in U.S. embassies around the world. During Ronald Reagan's presidency, Habib was appointed as special envoy to the Middle East, where he earned respect for defusing several crises.

Another prominent Arab American who was appointed to office is Donna Shalala. Of Lebanese descent, Shalala was born in Cleveland in 1941. After serving in the Peace Corps in Iran, Shalala earned her Ph.D. President Bill Clinton chose Shalala to be secretary of the Department of Health and Human Services, a post she held throughout Clinton's eight-year administration. During that time she was the highest-ranking Arab American appointed to office. Shalala expanded health care insurance to children, raised the rates of child immunizations, and oversaw the welfare reform process.

Arab Americans have also been voted into office. By the 1960s Arab Americans had won seats in the House of Representatives. Lebanese American James

Abourezk became the first Arab American senator, elected in 1972 from South Dakota. Abourezk's passionate interest in Arab Americans and American Middle East policy developed after a visit to his father's birthplace in Lebanon and a tour of the Middle East made in 1973. "What I heard there about the problems of the Middle East didn't seem to fit in at all

Philip Habib (left) served as special envoy to the Middle East under president Ronald Reagan.

with what I had been hearing in Washington. . . . I discovered I had been hearing just one side of the story,"[45] he said in an interview in 1982. In 1980 he founded the American-Arab Anti-Discrimination Committee to combat stereotyping of Arab Americans.

The first Arab American governor was Victor Aityeh, a Republican from Portland, Oregon, who was elected in 1978. Arab American senator George Mitchell, a Democrat from Maine whose mother Mary Saad was a factory worker, rose to the position of Senate majority leader in 1989. In the Senate, Mitchell was instrumental in winning passage of the Americans with Disabilities Act. John H. Sununu, a former Republican governor from New Hampshire, was appointed White House chief of staff under President George H.W. Bush. His son John E. Sununu is a senator from New Hampshire.

Arab American Activists

Arab American activists have made significant contributions to America's political and social life. Ralph Nader's impact on American political life has been immeasurable, even though he has never held an elected office or cabinet appointment. Nader was born in 1934 to Lebanese immigrants in a small town in Connecticut. As a free-lance journalist Nader became fascinated by the design of the American automobile. He claimed that the auto industry was making cars it knew to be unsafe in order to maximize its profits. In 1965 he published his ground-breaking book, *Unsafe at Any Speed: The Designed-in Dangers of the American Automobile.* The auto industry tried to discredit him, but Nader retaliated with a lawsuit, which he won.

Nader's efforts significantly changed the way in which automobiles are built. Not only did he force the auto industry to make cars safer, he also helped the American public to understand why safety features, like seat belts, are worth paying for. With the money Nader won in his legal suit, he went on to found the modern consumer movement. In 2000 Nader ran for president on the Green Party ticket, but garnered only a small percentage of the votes cast.

Another crusader for safety on the roads is Arab American Candy Lightner. After Lightner's twelve-year-old daughter was killed by a drunken driver, she founded Mothers Against Drunk Driving (MADD). Today the organization has chapters in all fifty states. Through her lectures and books Lightner has helped convince Americans that alcohol and driving do not mix. Americans owe much to Arab Americans for the cars they drive —both their manufacture and their safety features.

Entertainment and Sports

Arab Americans have also found success in virtually all fields of sports and entertainment. A familiar voice on the radio is that of Casey Kasem, whose crackling delivery of sports events, and his subsequent role as disc jockey, won him a place in the Broadcasting Hall of Fame. He was born in 1932 in Detroit, the son of Lebanese Druze parents. During his long career,

Arab Americans in the Military

Arab Americans have a long history of service in the American armed forces, beginning with World War I through today. By the time World War I ended in 1918, over thirteen thousand Syrian Americans had served in the U.S. Army, approximately 7 percent of the entire Syrian population in America. Ashad Hawie, a member of the 167th Alabama Infantry Regiment, was highly decorated for his feats of bravery in France and won the Croix de Guerre from the French as well as the U.S. Purple Heart.

It is difficult to know how many Americans of Arab descent fought in World War II because records of enlistment were not kept according to ethnic group. It is estimated that at least thirty thousand Arab Americans fought with U.S. forces. One star was Colonel James Jabara, America's first flying ace of the war. He went on to earn fame in the Korean War as America's first jet plane flying ace. Jabara was awarded two Distinguished Flying Crosses and was designated Most Distinguished Aviator by the Air Force Association.

In 2001 Arab Americans founded the Association of Patriotic Arab Americans in the Military, which is currently gathering information from Arab American veterans and servicemen about their service in the U.S. military. According to Jamal Baadani, who founded the group, ten thousand Muslims currently serve in the U.S. military, which in 1993 appointed its first Muslim chaplain. Baadani himself served in the Middle East, where he was posted to Lebanon in the 1980s.

Saade Mustafa recalled what joining the military meant to him: "I'm American, born and raised here. My parents are Palestinian. I've lived in Brooklyn all my life, except when I traveled with the U.S. Navy. I joined right after high school. . . . I served four months in the Persian Gulf. It was a big turning point in my life, figuring out who I was and what my religion meant to me, realizing that me and my parents come from different worlds," he said in an interview with *Saudi Aramco World* magazine in December 2001.

Lebanese American general John Abizaid was appointed commander of U.S. Central Command in Iraq following the 2003 war in Iraq. His fluent Arabic and his experience serving in northern Iraq following the Persian Gulf War of 1991 served him well in his new and important role in the Middle East.

which also includes acting, he has been actively engaged in supporting the Arab American community, especially through his efforts to stop the stereotyping of Arab Americans in the media.

Notable Arab Americans in sports include football players Jeff George, Bill George, and Abe Gibran, and coach Rich Kotite. Doug Flutie, who returned to playing football for the National Football

Activist Ralph Nader (right) joins singer Patti Smith (left) at a campaign rally. Of Lebanese descent, Nader ran for president in 2000.

League after playing in Canada, has a street named after him—"Flutie Pass"—in his hometown in Massachusetts. He founded the Doug Flutie Jr. Foundation for Autism after he found his son had the disorder. In baseball there is Joe Lahoud, who played with the Boston Red Sox.

Generations of Americans who watched TV in the 1950s and early 1960s fondly remember Arab American actor Danny Thomas, whose program *Make Room for Daddy* was a popular situation comedy with a traditional family setting. His daughter, Marlo Thomas, who was born in 1938, made her way in entertainment just as the feminist movement caught hold in the 1970s. She pioneered in creating the TV role of an independent and single woman in the series *That Girl*. Her record album, *Free to Be You and Me*, with memorable songs designed to fight gender stereotyping of both boys and girls, inspired a whole generation of young people to be all that they could be.

Arab Americans have also been rock stars, like the late Frank Zappa, Broadway actors like F. Murray Abraham, and directors like Julie Taymor, who created the famed Broadway production *The Lion King.* Character actor Tony Shalhoub has appeared on stage, TV, and in numerous films, including *Primary Colors, Big Night,* and *Searching for Bobby Fisher.* Shalhoub won a Golden Globe Award and an Emmy Award for best actor in 2003 for the comedy series *Monk.*

Alive in America: Arabic Music

Music is another area that has been touched by Arab Americans. In America, Arabic music was kept alive by the many professional musicians who came as immigrants in the early years of Arab immigration. They brought with them ancient melodies and instruments such as the oud and *sintir*, which are lutes; the *nay*, a reed flute; and the *qanoon*, a large zither.

Dancers dressed in traditional clothing perform to Arabic music at a local festival. Arabic music is enjoying a strong revival on the world music scene.

Not only did Arabic music survive in a new land, it infused the musical melting pot of America with new beats, melodies, and instruments. Drawing on ancient Arabic sounds, musicians today are able to create original compositions. The musicians who have made it in this scene are called "crossover artists" because they appeal to both Arab and American audiences.

American producers have been responsible for recording and mass marketing many of the artists. In 1981 David Byrne and Brian Eno (although not Arab American themselves) put out an influential album that blended a Lebanese folk lyric with a pulsating bass guitar. Another Arab American artist, Simon Shaheen, composed pieces for traditional Arab instruments using the undulating style of Arabic singing, which he then modified electronically.

Today, Arabic music is enjoying a revival on the world music scene as singers from a variety of Arab nations adapt ancient traditions to pop music. By far, the most popular new music is *rai*, sung primarily by North African recording stars and now very popular among Arab Americans and other American youth. In *rai* the songwriter digs deep into his or her personal feelings and sings them to explosive dance beats. Radios across many American cities now pulsate with the sinuous singing and rhythm of these new sounds.

Queen Noor

American-born Lisa Najeeb Halaby grew up in a distinguished Arab American family. She is the daughter of Najeeb Halaby, former chief executive of Pan American World Airways and former director of the Federal Aviation Administration. In 2002 she published her memoirs, *Leap of Faith: Memoirs of an Unexpected Life.*

Lisa Halaby was raised in Los Angeles and New York and graduated from the first coeducational class of Princeton University. Following in her father's footsteps, she became interested in working for the airline industry. After obtaining a degree in urban planning, she joined the Royal Jordanian Airline as director of planning and design projects.

Despite all her success, Halaby never dreamed she would become a queen. Through her work she met King Hussein of Jordan. In 1978, at the age of twenty-six, she married the king and became Noor al Hussein, queen of Jordan. She converted to Islam and with the king raised their four children. King Hussein died in 1999.

Since Lisa Halaby became Queen Noor, she has won wide acclaim for her humanitarian work within Jordan, which includes working for the protection of the environment, family health, women, and enterprise development. She has won international awards for efforts to promote peace in the Middle East. She chairs the King Hussein Foundation, a nonprofit organization.

Business and Science

From their earliest days in America, Arab Americans have been entrepreneurs who have started independent small businesses—restaurants, mom-and-pop grocery stores, and clothing stores. Many moved into the business of business itself, carving out fields in banking and accounting. Some Arab American entrepreneurs became highly successful. Gregory Orfalea, for example, founded the Kinko's copy stores in 1970, of which there are now over eleven hundred.

With Arab American workers heavily represented in the auto industry, it makes sense that some Arab Americans have made it to the very top of the industry. Jacques Nasser, who was born in Lebanon, is former president and chief executive officer of Ford Motor Company. Stephen Yokich, whose parents worked in the auto industry, rose to become president of the international United Auto Workers union.

One of the most prominent names in aviation is that of Najeeb E. Halaby, who is of Syrian and Lebanese descent. In the days of propeller airplanes, Halaby was one of the first Americans to test-fly the jet airplane during World War II. He went on to become the head of the Federal Aviation Administration and chief executive officer of Pan American World Airways. His daughter, Lisa Halaby, married the late King Hussein of Jordan. Halaby died in 2003.

Arab Americans are also prominent members of the scientific and medical communities. Dr. Michael DeBakey invented the heart pump. Egyptian-born Dr. Farouk el-Baz was instrumental in planning the Apollo moon landings. In order to study the earth from outside the earth's atmosphere, he pioneered the use of space photography. Arab American astronaut Christa McAuliffe gave her life to the exploration of outer space when the space shuttle *Challenger* exploded in 1986. McAuliffe was a teacher and in that capacity her mission continues; many schools are named in her memory throughout the United States.

Arab Americans have come far since they first arrived in their new home. They started off predominantly as peddlers, walking the continent on foot. Since then their efforts have helped America to pioneer the auto and airlines industries, and to soar into outer space.

CHAPTER SIX

Finding a Voice

Researchers have discovered an interesting thing about American attitudes toward Arabs. According to political scientist Michael W. Suleiman, if a person of Arab descent is identified according to his or her country of origin—as Lebanese or Egyptian, for example—few negative images are attached to the person. But if the same person is identified as an Arab, many more negative biases adhere to the person. The very word "Arab" comes with a lot of baggage in Western societies. Many people still imagine Arabs as Bedouin nomads roaming the desert on camels, even though Arab nations are filled with bustling, modern cities. Stereotypes persist of men as greedy oil sheiks, while women are typecast as either exotic belly dancers or oppressed wearers of *hijab*, the Muslim head covering.

In the 1980s, when a wave of terrorist activity erupted on the world scene, biased views of Arabs steadily increased. This resulted in a wave of hate crimes against Arab Americans, even as they attained prominent positions and economic success in American society. In the 1980s Arab Americans founded several organizations designed to combat negative images of Arabs in the media and to fight hate crimes. These moves strengthened the voice of the Arab American community while making Arab American contributions to American life more visible.

Arab Americans Become a Target

The 1980s saw numerous hijackings and kidnappings throughout the world, which spread fear among Americans. In 1979, for example, a group of Iranian students trying to overthrow the American-backed shah of Iran took over the American embassy in Tehran and held fifty-two people captive for 444 days. Many Americans felt a combination of rage and helplessness during this time.

In 1985 TWA Flight 847 was hijacked by a Lebanese gunman, who beat one American to death and held thirty-nine Americans hostage for seventeen days. In the same year the luxury cruise ship *Achille Lauro* made international headlines when it was hijacked by the Palestine Liberation Front. Of course, many acts of terror in the 1980s were also committed by terrorists who were not Arab, but when President Ronald Reagan announced his war against international terrorism, most Americans associated this with terrorism originating in the Middle East.

The public's growing fear of terrorist acts was fanned by constant news coverage of hijackings and hostage taking. Over the course of the decade, many Americans came to associate the word "Arab" with "terrorist" to such an extent that the two words were fused into one meaning. James J. Zogby, the founder of the Arab American Institute, writes that the American public "only saw one-dimensional stereotypical images, and because of the media's obsession with isolated violent acts . . . the terrorist was not seen as the exception to the Arab culture or the religion of Islam, but the rule."[46]

President Ronald Reagan (right) declared war on terrorism in the 1980s. Unfortunately, many Americans continue to equate Arabs with terrorists.

As Americans continued to be the victims of terrorist acts abroad and felt helpless to stop them, some vented their anger at Arab Americans. Others became irrationally fearful of anyone who "looked" Arab or Muslim on an airplane, for example.

Eventually this led some people to commit crimes of hate against Arab Americans. Mosques and Arab institutions became targets: In 1985 Islamic centers in California, Michigan, and Massachusetts were vandalized or received telephone threats. Failed bombing attempts and suspicious fires broke out in others. Similar incidents occurred in Texas and New York. Arab American community leaders received threatening phone calls. In other incidents, Arab students were harassed and beaten, and Arab-owned businesses were attacked and vandalized. In an interview, one Arab American woman from Iraq reported,

I am thinking that my whole life in the United States has been punctuated by nothing but misery and bad news of the Middle East. . . . And af-

---

James G. Abourezk Founds the American-Arab Anti-Discrimination Committee

In his book Advise and Dissent, *written in 1989, James Abourezk describes how he founded the ADC after he decided not to run for the U.S. Senate for a second term.*

In 1980, with [the anti-Arab scandal] Abscam on everyone's mind, it seemed to me to be the perfect time to try to organize people against anti-Arab racism. I called a meeting of several Arab-American leaders who were coming to Washington for a convention of the NAAA [National Association of Arab Americans], and presented to them the idea of establishing a separate organization to combat racism against people of Arab descent. There was no hesitation. Agreement was enthusiastic, and the American-Arab Anti-Discrimination Committee, or ADC, was born. . . .

In order to build ADC, I spent several years dragging myself from city to city throughout the United States haranguing audiences . . . and asking for their membership in the new grass-roots organization that I was forming. My efforts were successful. Membership surged during the [1982 Israeli] invasion of Lebanon, spurred by anger at the Israeli onslaught, but it continued to rise even after that. ADC has since blossomed into the largest and most politically aggressive American-Arab organization in the United States. It has brought together Arab Americans as well as non-Arab activists from virtually every part of America, making the Arab-American community aware of the political benefits of organization for the first time.

ter the wars [in the Middle East], the prejudice [in America] against us because we are Arabs and the whole media portrayal of "these terrorists." . . . My sons were beaten up in grade school and in high school because they were half Arab. My son says, "Sometimes I don't want to say I'm an Arab." I feel badly for children that they have to hide their identity.[47]

Rethinking Their Identity

The rising tide of hate crimes against Arab Americans challenged their ability to remain unified. Fearing prejudice, some Arab Americans no longer wanted to identify themselves as Arab. Some Christian descendants of first wave immigrants, assimilated into the American mainstream for almost a century, particularly wanted to distance themselves from being identified as Arab. On the other hand, some Muslim Arab Americans chose to emphasize their religious affiliation over their identity as Arabs. This was especially true of the more recently arrived Muslim Arabs. Because Islam encompasses a worldwide *ummah*, or community, they sought an overarching identity with other Muslims whether they were American converts or Muslim immigrants from a variety of Arab and non-Arab countries.

For other Arab Americans, however, fighting prejudice became a way to reassert their pride in their identity. To do so they formed a variety of organizations to represent themselves to the American public. These associations researched and published proud histories of Arab American communities across America, responded quickly to counter hate crimes, and asked Americans not to scapegoat their community.

Getting Politically Involved

One of the goals of the Arab American community was to change American perceptions about the Arab-Israeli conflict, and to win sympathy for the plight of the Palestinians. Arab Americans were united in the belief that the American news media so favored Israel that the public never had the chance to hear the other side of the story—the Palestinian side. To make their views heard, Arab Americans sought a stronger voice in the media and in government.

Finding effective means to assert themselves politically was not easy, however. Like other special interest groups in America, Arab Americans made financial contributions to candidates running for political office whose policies they either supported or wished to influence. But Arab Americans unhappily discovered that a variety of candidates refused to accept their contributions and endorsements. The American public at large was staunchly pro-Israel; and some American politicians did not want to alienate their Jewish supporters. An ill-informed public perceived Arab donations as being tainted by terrorist groups or bribes from rich oil magnates. Candidates were afraid to be associated with either.

In 1972, for example, presidential candidate George McGovern rejected an endorsement by Arab Americans. In 1980

Pro-Palestinian demonstrators march outside the White House in 1980. Arab Americans have had to struggle to gain a voice in American politics.

Jimmy Carter and Ronald Reagan both refused support from Arab American groups, although they did accept endorsements from those associated with specific countries, such as Lebanese Americans.

Arab Americans were further discouraged by a scandal of the early 1980s that came to be known as Abscam. Abscam was a political operation designed to unearth corrupt practices in Washington. Although Arabs had not been known to bribe U.S. congressmen, federal investigators disguised themselves as Arab sheiks and attempted to bribe members of Congress. The covert operation was called Abscam because it combined the words "Arab" and "scam." The fact that investigators chose to pose as Arabs exposed the low opinion the U.S. government held of Arabs in general.

When this shameful incident came to light, Arab Americans realized that they would need to do more to make their voices heard in America. In early 1980 former Arab American senator James Abourezk invited more than sixty Arab American leaders from around the country to a meeting in Washington, D.C. With their support, Abourezk established the American-Arab Anti-Discrimination Committee, or the ADC, which pledged to defend the civil rights of Arab Americans and fight biased news reporting in the media. The organization is in the forefront of the fight to counter discrimination against Arab Americans today.

Putting Arab Americans in Office

Gaining a greater voice for Arab Americans in U.S. politics has been another mission of Arab American organizations, especially the Arab American Institute, founded by James J. Zogby in the mid-1980s. Zogby's goal was to support the candidacies of qualified Arab Americans, from the local to federal level, whether Democratic or Republican. The effort to bring more Arab Americans into the political arena started to pay off. Among the Arab Americans elected to office was Mary Rose Oakar, who represented Ohio in the U.S. House of Representatives from 1977 to 1993. She now serves as head of the American-Arab Anti-Discrimination Committee. Spencer Abraham served as chairman of the Michigan Republican Party in the 1980s, and as senator from Michigan from 1995 to 2001. Subsequently he was appointed by George W. Bush to be secretary of energy.

Another breakthrough for Arab Americans was that candidates finally accepted the backing of Arab American support groups. In 1984 presidential nominees Jesse Jackson and Ronald Reagan both did so. In the 1988 presidential candidacy of Jesse Jackson, the African American civil rights leader, Arab Americans finally found a major U.S. politician who urged that America open up talks directly with the Palestine Liberation Organization.

(Left to right) Maher Abdelqader, Ziad Asali, and James Zogby field questions during a 2002 press conference. Each leads an Arab American political organization.

This is something the U.S. government eventually did do.

Combating Anti-Arab Prejudice in the Media

Another goal of Arab American organizations was to combat anti-Arab prejudice in the media. Negative images on TV and in the movies can have a powerful cumulative effect on public opinion about who Arabs are and what they are like. Arab Americans are rarely portrayed as ordinary folks; instead they are represented as what some critics have called the three B's—as billionaires, bombers, and belly dancers.

The sources of anti-Arab stereotypes in the media date back to the 1920s when Arabs were portrayed in the movies as exotic and scary strangers. In the 1920s Rudolph Valentino, the popular film star, played an Arab in *The Sheik* and *Son of the Sheik*. These movies, viewed by millions of Americans, portrayed Arabs as lustful and often violent. In another popular movie of the 1930s, Tarzan rescues Jane from an evil Arab kidnapper. More recently, cartoon characters such as Batman fend off hoards of Arab invaders, and computer games now present Arabs as an evil force that must be conquered. Action films like *Delta Force* (1986) and *The Siege* (1998) continue in this tradition.

The Disney film *Aladdin* (1992) did present an Arab as its hero, but upon more careful inspection, many Arab Americans were upset by its portrayal of their homelands. The film's opening song presents a negative view of Arab lands:

Oh, I come from a land,
From a faraway place
Where the caravan camels roam.
Where they cut off your ear
If they don't like your face.
It's barbaric, but hey, it's home.[48]

After viewing the film Arab American activist Candy Lightner wrote, "I was angry and embarrassed when I listened to the *Aladdin* lyrics while watching the movie. I could only hope that the audience was not paying close attention and would not take home with them a poor image of the Arab world."[49]

Arab American advocacy groups have had some success at eliminating stereotypes such as these in the entertainment media. For example, because of Arab American protests, Disney finally agreed to change some of the offensive words in the opening song of its video version of *Aladdin.* To keep Hollywood on its toes, the ADC and other Arab American organizations publish critiques of movies and TV programs that defame Arabs and Arab Americans.

It has been much more difficult for Arab Americans to fight what they perceive to be biased reporting about the Middle East in the news media. A case in point was newspaper and television coverage of Iraq between the 1991 and 2003 Persian Gulf wars when United Nations sanctions were in place. The sanctions put a trade embargo on Iraq, forbidding all exports and imports to and from Iraq except humanitarian aid. During this time the U.S. news media focused on Saddam Hussein's totalitarian government and the weapons of mass destruction thought to exist in Iraq. There was little coverage, however, of the enormous suffering the sanctions caused the Iraqi people, which may have claimed the lives of hundreds of thousands of Iraqi children. The faces of ordinary Arabs thus disappeared as the news focused on terror and tyrants.

Arab American organizations have responded to such news reporting by publishing written critiques of specific newscasts, but these have generally been ineffective in changing the perspective of news agencies. The websites set up by many Arab American organizations have been more effective in presenting to the American public alternative reporting and interpretation of events in the Middle East.

Fighting Hate Crimes and Discrimination

Beginning in the 1980s, the ADC began to document and publicize hate crimes committed against Arab Americans. In its *1991 Report on Anti-Arab Hate Crimes*, the ADC reported crimes such as these: "01/13/91—San Diego, CA. *Attempted bombing:* A homemade bomb was discovered in the restroom of a San Diego mosque during Friday prayers. The device did not explode. . . . 01/17/91—Providence, RI. *Harassing letter:* A harassing letter was sent to an Arab American: 'You are nothing but a traitor to your country. Go back to Syria where you belong before you get hurt.'"[50] Acts of intimidation, vandalism, and physical violence also seemed to increase to coincide with tumultuous

The Murder of Alex Odeh

The violence against Arab Americans in the 1980s reached its peak with the murder of Alex Odeh in 1985. Odeh, who was forty-one at the time of his death, was western regional director of the American-Arab Anti-Discrimination Committee in California. On October 11 someone booby-trapped a bomb to the door of his office, killing him instantly.

At the time of his murder, the news media were filled with accounts of the hijacking of the cruise liner the *Achille Lauro* by Arab terrorists. Some speculate that Odeh was killed by a non-Arab seeking revenge for the *Achille Lauro*, even though Odeh was not affiliated with terrorism and had publicly condemned the attack. It still rankles the Arab American community that his death received little news coverage by the U.S. media at the time and that his killing remains unsolved. In memory of the slain rights activist, the Alex Odeh Memorial Statue was erected in Santa Ana City, California, in 1994.

events in the Middle East. For example, the ADC recorded thirty-nine hate crimes in all of 1990, but more than forty in just the first week of the Persian Gulf War of 1991. The growing evidence of a pattern of hate crimes put pressure on Congress to investigate anti-Arab racism. The

Subcommittee on Criminal Justice, led by Congressman John Conyers, opened hearings in 1986 for the first time about this problem.

Since then politicians and the U.S. Congress have actively condemned anti-Arab violence. For example, during the Persian Gulf War, President George H.W. Bush said, "Death threats, physical attacks, vandalism, religious violence and discrimination against Arab-Americans must end. These hate crimes have no place in a free society and we are not going to stand for them."[51] During the war the vast majority of Americans stood by their Arab American neighbors. For example, Sam Yono, an Iraqi who owns video and grocery stores in the Greater Detroit area, reported, "I was astonished at the sympathy for us during the war. . . . People would ask about our relatives back in Iraq. There were some unpleasant remarks, but the majority of people were concerned."[52]

"Some People Are Scared of a Scarf"

Arab American organizations have also fought many forms of discrimination against Arab Americans at school and at work. The wearing of *hijab*, for example, has caused problems for Muslim women

A Sikh leader lists reasons for racial prejudice during a diversity training program. Americans often lump together Sikhs, Hindus, Muslim and non-Muslim Arabs.

who are sometimes denied jobs because they wear a head covering. One Iraqi Muslim woman complained that Americans view her head scarf as a sign that she is either an oppressed woman or a terrorist. "Some ignorant people are scared of a scarf,"[53] she said in an interview with the *New York Times*. The ADC has documented cases where girls have had their head coverings ripped off in school and been beaten.

Arab men have similarly faced harassment at work when colleagues called them, even in jest, terrorists. In other cases Arab Americans have complained that they have not been hired, or have been fired, because of their ethnic background. Arab Americans have also faced discrimination in the form of racial profiling, at airport screenings for example. In these proceedings people are singled out for inspection or detained not because of anything they have done, but because their ethnic backgrounds or their appearance matches a profile of people authorities are trying to catch.

Arab American organizations offer help to those complaining of such abuses by informing them of their rights. Immigrants new to America may not know that federal law prohibits discrimination based on national origin, race, and religion or that the United States guarantees freedom of religion and therefore the right of women to wear *hijab*. Arab American organizations like the ADC inform members of the community about their rights and how they can contact civil rights lawyers who will help them seek justice.

Taking Pride in Heritage

By the turn of the twenty-first century, Arab Americans had much to celebrate about their history of success in America, but few other Americans knew about their accomplishments. To preserve the Arab American past, historians of the community and organizations like the ADC set out to document it.

The goal of the ADC was to record the history of representative Arab American communities across America. This took painstaking research, including extensive interviewing of the oldest generation still living. Through this effort many Arab American families began to take an interest in their own stories. In the introduction to *Taking Root, Bearing Fruit*, James Zogby writes that the authors "put our best foot forward by presenting selected vignettes about our families and neighborhoods, our institutions, leaders and friends—in short our culture and our tradition. Sit back, enjoy the reading, and above all, be proud of who you are."[54] The Naff Arab American Collection, held at the Smithsonian Institution in Washington, D.C., reflects similar work. It includes 450 oral interviews and several thousand photographs that document the Arab American experience.

The effort to record the Arab American past and to make it more visible to other Americans continues with the founding of the Arab American National Museum, slated to open in Dearborn, Michigan. It will narrate the history of the community in America and celebrate its successes. Many of the objects that will go on display are being donated by Arab American families, including family photographs, documents such as letters and old newspapers, personal belongings, and works of art and film.

A Unified Voice for a Multifaceted Community

It has not always been easy or even possible for Arab Americans to find a unified voice about the complex issues facing America. This has been especially true regarding recent crises in the Middle East. Because Arab Americans trace their roots to so many different Arab countries—countries that may even be at war with one another—Arab Americans sometimes find themselves on opposing sides of an issue.

The Persian Gulf War of 1991 was one such difficult time for Arab Americans. Arab countries themselves were divided over whether or not to support the American-led coalition to repel the Iraqi invasion of Kuwait. A spokesperson for the National Association of Arab Americans reported at the time, "This is one of the most emotional crises in the history of our community. . . . The people have become very polarized."[55] Most Iraqi Americans were not in favor of the U.S.-led invasion and wanted to give diplomacy a longer chance to work at getting Iraq out of Kuwait. Thousands of Iraqi Americans had relatives in Iraq, and they feared for their safety.

Kuwaiti Americans, on the other hand, were in favor of the war because it was their country that had been invaded by Iraq. An engineering student at George Wash-

The Oklahoma City Bombing and Arab Americans

When newscasters took to the airwaves to report the Oklahoma City terrorist attack of 1995, the Arab American community became painfully aware of how many Americans viewed Arabs. In the attack a federal office building in Oklahoma City was destroyed by a car bomb, killing 168 people. The Oklahoma City bombing was the deadliest terrorist attack America had yet witnessed. Within hours of the crime, many experts said that all signs pointed to its having been committed by Muslim Arab terrorists. With no evidence at hand, many Americans were ready to reach the same conclusion.

A mere two days later, the police caught the lead culprit: twenty-six-year-old Timothy McVeigh, a U.S. Army veteran and member of a white racist paramilitary group. He was later tried and executed. In their rush to judgment, politicians, the news media, and many ordinary Americans came face-to-face with the prejudices they held about Arabs and Muslims. The tragic Oklahoma City bombing taught America that terrorism has no race, nationality, or religion to which it can be attributed.

Kuwaitis cheer U.S. troops who liberated Kuwait from Iraq in 1991. America's military involvement in the Mideast has been a divisive issue for Arab Americans.

ington University from Kuwait said at the time, "Although we regret that there is a military option used here, we believe that all other options have been exhausted."[56]

Although there was no way to unify all Arab Americans on this issue, it was nonetheless helpful to have organizations that could present the public face of the community. The Arab American Institute condemned Iraq, supported President George H.W. Bush as well as the United Nations resolutions, but stopped short of supporting a U.S.-led invasion of Iraq. This was a position that most Arab Americans could probably support. Organizations like the Arab American Institute poll Arab Americans to find out what they are

thinking on any given issue. Knowing the results of a poll can help both leaders of the Arab American community and U.S. politicians learn what Arab Americans are thinking, and therefore better respond to their concerns and needs.

Overall the adversity faced by the Arab American community in recent decades has not weakened it, but rather strengthened it. Through the need to confront anti-Arab bias and hate crimes and the desire to influence American foreign policy, Arab Americans established organizations through which they could fight for their rights, strengthen group pride, and raise a voice loud enough to be reckoned with in the American political system.

CHAPTER SEVEN

Facing the Future

On September 1, 2001, the U.S. Postal Service issued its first stamp in Arabic. The stamp was the brainchild of a Muslim fifth grader, Muhib Beekun, who realized in 1996 that the U.S. Postal Service issued stamps honoring Christmas, Hanukkah, and Kwanzaa, but no stamp recognizing the two Muslim eids, or celebrations, one that ends the fast at Ramadan and the other that concludes the hajj.

The stamp has a blue background. In its center rests beautiful Arabic calligraphy that says *id mubarak*, or "blessed feast." In English appear the words "Eid Greetings." The newly issued eid stamp repre-sents America's acknowledgment that Islam now constitutes an important part of the American landscape. It is estimated that there are now more than 6 million Muslims in the United States. After the first-day-of-issue ceremony, one Muslim student said, "*Now* I feel like an Ameri-can."[57]

At the beginning of the new millen-nium, Arab Americans could look back at over one hundred years of prosperity, achievement, and recognition for their many contributions to American life. Yet ten days after the U.S. Postal Service is-sued the eid stamp, Arab Americans were confronted with a host of new problems arising from the tragic events of September 11, 2001.

The Impact of September 11, 2001, on Arab Americans

On September 11, 2001, two hijacked planes crashed into the Twin Towers of the World Trade Center in New York City. Little more than several hours later, both buildings cascaded to the ground in a sea of smoldering dust. A third hijacked plane smashed into the Pentagon in Washington, D.C., while a fourth plane crashed into the Pennsylvania countryside. Nearly three thousand people died in one of the most tragic events in the nation's history.

It was quickly confirmed that all nineteen of the hijackers were Muslim Arabs, fifteen of them from Saudi Arabia. All belonged to an international terrorist network known as al-Qaeda. Even though Islam forbids suicide and the murder of innocent victims, the terrorists claimed that their actions were sanctioned by their faith.

Arab American and American Muslim leaders immediately and publicly condemned the attacks of September 11, in no uncertain terms. The American-Arab Anti-Discrimination Committee said, "Arab Americans, like all Americans, are shocked and angered by such brutality, and we share all the emotions of our fellow citizens. Arab Americans view these attacks as targeting all Americans without exception."[58] This statement, released to the news media, made it clear that Arab Americans viewed themselves as Americans first. They were not on the sidelines of these events, but like all Americans, had been victimized by them. Islamic organizations seconded this sentiment: "[We condemn] in the harshest terms the senseless acts of terror perpetrated against innocent American citizens. . . . This tragedy affects all of us Americans, and we should do whatever we can to help,"[59] said the Islamic Institute.

The eid stamp, commemorating Muslim holidays, was issued on September 1, 2001.

Contributing to the Rescue Efforts

Like so many Americans, Arab Americans lost loved ones in the tragedy. They also served in the rescue mission. Among the many who helped were firefighter Ali Taqi, who unloaded supplies and searched for victims at Ground Zero, and Dr. Taufik Kassis, who treated the wounded. Saade Mustafa, a Palestinian American, remembers what it was like to be part of a rescue team in the days following the tragedy:

A lighting company had a truck going to Ground Zero and I said, "I want to go there." I was overwhelmed just to be down there, to breathe that air. But in the midst of the horror there was beauty. Everybody was just so caring, so giving. . . . I wish we could have saved everybody. I just wanted to do my part as a New Yorker, as a fellow human being.[60]

As firefighters from other parts of the country came to New York's aid, so did Iraqi American Ron Kuley, who spent seven weeks in New York as part of a group from Virginia. The Islamic Institute and the American-Arab Anti-Discrimination Committee honored Kuley along with the rescue efforts of Arab Americans Adil Almontaser, Rafet Awad, Faisal Khan, and Ahmed Nasser, all members of the New York Police Department.

Arab Americans Remember September 11

Arab Americans Rasmieh Abed and her daughter Sana Abed participated in one of the many candlelight marches held throughout New York City in the days following September 11. In an article that appeared in *Saudi Aramco World* magazine in December 2001, Rasmieh Abed recalled what she felt like that day.

"My thoughts on that day were that I love America. That's why I was holding the flag. We love this country. We've made it our home. My relatives came here 60 years ago. My grandfathers, my uncles, my mother's uncles and my father's uncles lived and died in America. . . . Things are not good now between Arabs and America. I just want us to be united again, without any more fear. I was happy that we had all come together [at the demonstration] but inside, in my heart, I was still sad. It's not the same without the twin towers. The site was beautiful. Now the buildings are just gone. There's nothing there—just an empty space."

Her daughter, Sana, said: "We all felt so hurt and so sad. I wanted to show everybody that Arabs want peace. I seen us Arabs and Americans together that day [of the march]. Everybody was just together. One Jewish lady, she wore a scarf on her head to show support. There was American Muslim women wearing scarves on their heads. They all came so we could stand together."

In the aftermath of the tragedy, many Arab American organizations and individuals worked to raise money for the relief efforts. One of these was the Southern Federation of Syrian Lebanese American Clubs, which raised and donated twenty thousand dollars to the Twin Towers Orphan Fund. On behalf of the ADC, ninety thousand dollars was contributed to a fund to help the families of victims of September 11. The Arab Bankers Association of North America also donated funds, sending their money to the New York City Firefighters 9/11 Relief Fund.

Arab Americans also helped efforts to secure America's safety after the attacks. According to the U.S. Department of State, their aid was much appreciated: "FBI Director Robert S. Mueller thanked the Arab-American community and individuals who responded to his September 17 appeal for linguists with an 'overwhelming' flood of calls to the Bureau in Washington."[61] A year and a half later, Mueller addressed the American Muslim Council and praised the leaders of the American Muslim community for their continuing help: "[You] have taken the time to talk with our agents and support professionals to help them better understand Muslim perspectives and Muslim beliefs. In some cases, Arab American newspapers have even provided us with useful information."[62]

A Double Pain

As hard as it was for all Americans after September 11, Arab Americans faced special problems. The attacks had the effect of making Arab Americans feel that they had to defend themselves to their fellow Americans, by disavowing any connection to the attacks and reasserting their loyalty to America. It also wounded the community's sense of pride. One Lebanese American woman struggled with her wounded self-image just days after the attack. "I'm Arab, but if the Arabs did it, then I'm ashamed. . . . But if some Arabs did it, you can't say all Arabs are bad."[63]

Because the attackers were Arab Muslims who defended what they did in the name of Islam, Muslim Arabs had a second burden to bear: the pain of having to defend their faith. Most Americans knew little about Islam, and what they knew was often filled with stereotypes about Islam being a "religion of the sword" or a violent, fundamentalist faith. Arab American and other Muslims took the initiative to teach Americans about Islam, so the public would not believe that such acts of terror were sanctioned by their faith.

The feelings of many Arab Muslim students were summed up by Samar Ali, a student at Vanderbilt University who later became president of the student body:

Several people have asked me how I feel as an Arab-American Muslim. When I saw my country's buildings come tumbling down with thousands of my fellow citizens on Tuesday, I felt angry as an American at whoever did this. . . . The other part of me felt upset as a Muslim. I thought, "My God, did somebody really do this in the name of my religion? I want everyone to know that Arabs and

Arab Americans protest the law passed after the September 11, 2001, terrorist attacks requiring Muslim and Arabic aliens to register with immigration authorities.

Muslims around the world condemn this act."[64]

A Tense Tolerance

In addition to these problems, Arab Americans lived in fear that Americans would vent their anger at anyone who "looked" Arab or Muslim. Some Arab Americans were worried that their neighbors would no longer trust them, fearing they were terrorists or had secret terrorist ties. Many Muslim women were afraid to walk outside wearing their head scarves. Arab-owned restaurants and businesses were quick to display the American flag in their windows, lest anyone question their loyalty to America.

These fears were not unwarranted: In the month following the terrorist attacks, four hundred acts of violence against Arab Americans were recorded by the Arab American Institute. These included the murder of several Arab Americans in different regions of the country. In Cleveland, Ohio, a car was driven into the doorway of a mosque. Across the country, incidents of verbal and physical abuse skyrocketed.

The U.S. government tried to ease this tense situation for Arab Americans. "From the White House to the FBI to the Justice Department, it was emphasized early and often that hate crimes and discrimination would not be tolerated,"[65] writes author Michael S. Lee. Days after the attack, President George W. Bush spoke at the Islamic Center in Washington, D.C., and said, "America counts millions of Muslims amongst our citizens, and Muslims make an incredibly valuable contribution to our country. . . . And they need to be treated with respect. In our anger and emotion, our fellow Americans must treat each other with respect."[66]

In further efforts, Arab American leaders were invited to meet with members of Congress to promote useful strategies for assuring both the nation's security and the safety of the Arab American community. In 2003 the FBI established the Arab American Advisory Committee to which it appointed many leaders of the community. The committee provided a means for Arab Americans to aid FBI investigations into terrorism. If Arab Americans found that FBI investigative techniques unfairly targeted the Arab American community, they could contact the committee to protest.

Another thing that eased the isolation of Arab Americans was the number of interfaith gatherings held in communities across America. When a mosque in Columbus, Ohio, was vandalized, nearby churches and a synagogue offered their facilities for use by their Muslim neighbors. At an interfaith service in Washington, D.C., Cardinal Theodore McCarrick said, "It's important that we pray with our Muslim brothers. . . . There are some people that are really starting to take the wrong attitude,

New York police guard a mosque after the World Trade Center attacks. Nearly four hundred acts of violence against Arab Americans following the attacks were documented.

and looking at [Muslims] as lesser or hateful people. I think it's important that we put our arms around our Muslim brothers and sisters right now, and they know we love them, and they know we care."[67]

Local advertising campaigns also came to the aid of besieged Arab Americans. In a small town in Pennsylvania, an Egyptian-run diner found itself with no customers after rumors circulated that the owners were connected to the September 11 attacks. After a local newspaper wrote about the plight of the Egyptian proprietors, local residents returned to eat at the diner in force.

The Future of Arab Immigration

While efforts to stem the tide of anti-Arab violence in America were on the whole successful, the Arab American community faced other problems as a result of new immigration procedures undertaken by the government. In the years preceding September 11, the U.S. government had grown lax about implementing immigration policy, letting visitors overstay their visas without investigating their whereabouts, for example. Others arrived illegally to begin with. The government was embarrassed that the September 11 hijackers had been legally permitted to enter the United States, despite the fact that several were on lists of known terrorists. Some had lived in America under fake identities for months, unnoticed by authorities, while they attended U.S. flight schools, all the while plotting terror.

To root out possible terrorists living in the United States, the U.S. Congress approved the USA PATRIOT Act in October of 2001. The name of the act stands for Uniting and Strengthening America by Providing Appropriate Tools Required to Intercept and Obstruct Terrorism. The PATRIOT Act gives the government unusually broad powers to detain and deport aliens, based on little evidence, if they are thought to pose a threat to the security of the United States.

The government's new policy of asking visitors living in the United States to register with immigration officials has been applied selectively. Thus far it has targeted immigrants from Egypt, Jordan, Kuwait, Saudi Arabia, Sudan, Libya, Iran, Iraq, and other predominantly Muslim countries both within and beyond the Middle East, like Indonesia. Since September 11 thousands of Middle Eastern men have been detained by the Department of Justice or questioned by the FBI for no discernible reason other than their ethnic origin.

While some point out that it is reasonable to slow immigration from countries whose citizens are known to harbor anti-American sentiments, critics claim this is a form of racial profiling because people are subjected to investigation merely on the basis of where they come from or how they look. These policies have hit especially hard at foreign students from Arab countries studying at American universities, and experts expect that fewer of them will choose to study in America in the future.

In further efforts to weed out terrorists in 2003, over one hundred thousand male immigrants from Middle Eastern coun-

Arab American families hold a press conference at a community center to protest the deportation of family members in the immigration crackdown after the attacks.

tries were questioned in immigration offices. Although they registered voluntarily, nine thousand of these were found to be here illegally because of inconsistencies in their legal papers. They are now facing deportation proceedings. Of all those questioned, only eleven had suspected ties to terrorists. These procedures offended many men who felt their integrity was unfairly questioned by the government. "I love America so I have to respect the law. But we are not terrorists. We are coming here as law-abiding people to work,"[68] said Sameh, a car parking attendant, in an interview with the *New York Times*.

The fear of being deported has created a crisis for immigrants from Arab countries. Many of the illegal immigrants who came forward to register hoped that their demonstration of loyalty and cooperation with U.S. authorities would win them leniency. This has not proved to be the case, and the situation has taken its toll on Arab and Muslim communities. As Rachel L. Swarns reports: "Quietly the fabric of their neighborhoods is thinning. Families are packing up, and some are splitting up. Rather than come forward and risk deportation, an unknowable number of immigrants have burrowed deeper underground.

Others have simply left—for Canada or for home."[69]

Another plan designed to prevent terrorists from slipping into the United States is to curb the number of refugees coming from all Middle Eastern countries except for Israel. The United States has always been a beacon of hope to people from around the world fleeing oppression, and so this restriction has been controversial. Beginning in 2003, all asylum seekers from countries where al-Qaeda or other terrorist organizations are known to operate will be automatically detained for questioning for up to six months. This measure is likely to result in fewer Arab refugees seeking and gaining entrance to the United States in upcoming years, thus greatly reducing Arab immigration.

Investigating Mosques

Other actions taken by the government have focused on Arab and Muslim associations. After September 11, 2001, the U.S. government claimed that some of the largest Muslim charities, unbeknownst to their donors, were channeling their funds to terrorist organizations. These charities had their assets frozen by the U.S. gov-

Immigrants in Time of War

Arab Americans are not the first immigrant group to experience the United States at war with their homeland. During World War I and World War II, when the United States was fighting Germany, the loyalty of German Americans was questioned. As a consequence, many Germans Americanized their names—from Heinrich to Henry, for example—and stopped speaking German out of fear they would be viewed as sympathizers with the enemy, or even worse, spies.

America's treatment of its Japanese citizens during World War II has left a deep stain on the nation's conscience. After Japan attacked Pearl Harbor in 1941, more than 110,000 Japanese living along the West Coast were rounded up and placed in internment camps in inaccessible areas, such as the deserts of Arizona. Entire families were relocated and forced to live in the camps for the duration of the war. Most of them were U.S. citizens.

Just the fear that Japanese Americans might commit acts of espionage or sabotage was enough to convince Americans that this drastic and unconstitutional policy was justified. None of the internees was ever charged with a crime. Their homes and property were never returned to them.

Now it is Arab Americans whose loyalties are tested by the war on terrorism. While the United States has acknowledged the wrongs it inflicted on its Japanese citizens during World War II, the past nonetheless haunts Americans and adds a resonance of fear to the situation confronting Arab Americans today.

ernment. This put Muslims, for whom *zakat*, or the giving of charity, is a religious duty, in a bind. Not knowing whom to trust, and fearful of being branded a supporter of terrorism, many donors instead gave their gifts to the local soup kitchens of their neighborhood mosques, where they could see how their money was actually being used.

In 2003 the FBI continued its scrutiny of Arab American Muslims when it asked its local offices to count all mosques and Muslims living within their jurisdictions. The FBI gave conflicting accounts as to why it issued this measure. According to some agents, the count served to merely help agents to ensure the safety of mosques in the face of anti-Islamic prejudice. Other officials indicated that the count was designed to put pressure on FBI agents to be more vigilant about investigating mosques within their jurisdictions, whether or not they have shown signs of harboring Islamic terrorists. Whatever the reason, this effort has made law-abiding Muslims who were freely practicing their religion feel like suspects. It upset civil rights advocates, members of Congress, and Arab Americans. Members from all three groups have asked the FBI to rescind the order.

Arab American organizations have an important role to play in the debate about how to best ensure America's security without unduly compromising the rights of individual citizens. While supporting many of the government's antiterrorist measures, Arab American organizations have effectively registered their protests over policies that single out Arab Americans and Muslims, based on their ethnicity or religion, calling these policies a form of racial profiling and an invasion of privacy of all Americans. Their protests have been joined by other groups of Americans, including librarians and the American Civil Liberties Union, which is bringing a suit against provisions of the USA PATRIOT Act.

A Heightened Interest in Arab Americans

Since September 11, 2001, and the War in Iraq of 2003, U.S. newspapers have been filled with news about Arab countries. This has had many unexpected consequences for the Arab American community, not all of them negative. One positive consequence is that Americans have shown a sharply increased desire to learn more about Arab countries, Islam, and their Arab American neighbors.

Arab Americans have played a leading role in the effort to teach Americans about Arab civilization and Islam, whether they are professors of Arabic studies, members of Arab American organizations, imams and other religious leaders, students at universities, or the parents of children in public schools. The Islamic Networks Group made themselves available to teachers wishing to learn more about Islam. It now has speakers' bureaus in twenty-five cities. According to the *New York Times*, "The speakers originally lectured about Islam mostly in public schools . . . but in recent months [of 2003], the group has been flooded with invitations to explain the religion to police departments, groups for the elderly, community centers and Rotary Clubs."[70]

Workers pack up assets from the Holy Land Foundation, a Muslim charity the FBI accused of supporting terrorist organizations.

Organizations like the Arab American Institute and the Council on Islamic Education were quick to post special information packets on their websites after September 11, so that the general public as well as teachers could access accurate and up-to-date information. The Arab American Institute found that its website "hits" more than doubled.

Individuals have also undertaken efforts to make a difference. Palestinian American Samira Hussein, for example, teaches about her culture and religion at her daughter's school in Montgomery County, Maryland. "People didn't know much about Islam and Arabic history—they don't know that Muslims invented algebra and the compass. . . . So I decided that education was the best way to handle it,"[71] explained Hussein in a magazine interview. Soon after September 11, 2001, she was invited to speak about her work on National Public Radio.

Arab Americans are also in demand as teachers of Arabic. Whether Americans want to set up businesses in the Middle East, gather strategic information, communicate with Iraqi citizens about their future, or write for American broadcasts aimed at a Middle Eastern audience, a working knowledge of Arabic is essential. The importance the Middle East holds in the future peace and prosperity of the world, along with the lack of Arabic speakers working for the U.S. government, has made Arabic speakers in high demand.

Arab Americans and the War in Iraq

The 2003 war in Iraq presented Arab Americans with the dilemma of whether or not to support the U.S. invasion of Iraq. President George W. Bush initiated the war to destroy Iraqi weapons of mass destruction believed at the time to exist, and to oust dictator Saddam Hussein from power. Organizations like the American-Arab Anti-Discrimination Committee did not support America's invasion of Iraq. Like many countries around the world, most Arab Americans wanted to give UN inspectors more time to search for weapons of mass destruction.

Iraqi Americans were particularly torn about the best course of action. Even though they had suffered greatly at the hands of Saddam Hussein, they still had relatives in Iraq, and they feared for their safety in a U.S.-led invasion. Iraqi Americans

---

War in Iraq

The 2003 war in Iraq was related to the Persian Gulf War of 1991. At the conclusion of the first war, Iraq agreed to destroy all of its weapons of mass destruction, including biological, chemical, and nuclear weapons. UN teams of inspectors were charged with inspecting Iraq on a periodic basis to ensure that it was complying with this agreement. Beginning in 1998, however, President Saddam Hussein refused to let UN inspectors into his country.

In 2001 President George W. Bush asserted that Saddam Hussein posed a growing threat to the United States. He claimed that Iraq was continuing to develop weapons of mass destruction and that the United States could not wait to be attacked; rather it had to attack Iraq first. He also claimed that Saddam Hussein's government supported al-Qaeda, the terrorist organization that masterminded the attacks of September 11, 2001, although no direct link between the two was ever proved. Many other nations, along with some Ameri-cans, argued that such a preemptive war would violate international law.

The United States tried to win the approval of the UN Security Council to wage war against Iraq. It failed to win this approval, in part because Iraq had agreed to let the UN inspectors back into the country. Countries like France, Germany, and Russia wanted to avert war by giving the inspectors more time to see if Iraq had indeed destroyed its weapons of mass destruction.

In March 2003 the United States invaded Iraq and declared victory on April 14. Iraqis were happy to have Saddam Hussein's government ousted from power, but few welcomed the occupying U.S. forces. Even though the war was officially over, U.S. forces continued to be dogged by snipers who killed U.S. soldiers. Although work began to rebuild the infrastructure of Iraq and to establish a new government, it remained unclear whether Iraq could successfully be turned into the democratic ally the Bush administration claimed it could be.

President Bush chats with a Muslim leader near Detroit. Bush enlisted the help of Iraqi exiles living in the United States to rebuild Iraq after Saddam Hussein was toppled.

Sabiha Hakkak and her husband Hassan, for example, expressed feelings that were shared by other Americans of Iraqi descent before the war began. Mr. Hakkak said of the impending war with Iraq: "I support Bush to kick out Saddam and his group. . . . I don't support Iraqi civilians and American soldiers being killed. . . . But I don't know how they can avoid it."[72] When U.S. officials declared the invasion a success in March 2003, Iraqi Americans took to the streets of Detroit to celebrate, although few other Arab Americans did so.

After Saddam Hussein was toppled, American officials sought the help of Iraqi

exiles living in America to rebuild their country, and many had much to offer. A group of highly educated Iraqis met in Detroit with U.S. government officials, including at one point President Bush. The United States hoped that these Iraqis would be useful in the transition from an American-led occupation of Iraq to a new self-governing Iraq.

Iraqi Americans are in a good position to help the United States learn more about the needs of the Iraqi people, while teaching Iraqis about what it means to live in a democratic society, assuming their help is welcomed by the Iraqi people. According to the *New York Times*, "Those who plan to head [to Iraq] say they hope to use their fluent Arabic to translate for American soldiers and international humanitarian aid workers. . . . But perhaps most important, they say they hope to build a bridge between the culture they grew up in and the one that gave them refuge, teaching people who have suffered under tyranny how to live free."[73]

A Bridge Between Two Worlds

Arab Americans have other important roles to play in shaping the American future, especially in U.S. foreign policy. Many Arab Americans have lived in the Middle East or travel there regularly. Because they know both American and Arab culture, they are in a good position to help America build the bridges so necessary to world peace.

Secretary of State Colin Powell addressed the ADC in 2003 and acknowledged the importance of this role for the Arab American community:

> You are a vital bridge for understanding between Arabs and Americans, at home and abroad. . . . With a foot in both worlds, you have special insights into America and the Arab world, and a special responsibility to share your wisdom across cultural boundaries. I salute you for doing just that—for speaking out for peace in the Middle East and against intolerance within our borders.[74]

Arab Americans have been invited by the government to join a number of initiatives regarding peace in the Middle East. During the presidency of Bill Clinton, Arab American organizations were welcomed to the White House for discussions about a peace settlement. In 1993 Vice President Al Gore invited one hundred Arab Americans and Jewish Americans to be on the board of Builders for Peace. In 2003 George R. Salem and James Zogby of the Arab American Institute were appointed to the U.S. Advisory Commission on Public Diplomacy. The group was called into being to advise the Bush administration on ways to improve U.S. diplomacy in the Middle East.

Toward the Future

Arab Americans have come a long way in making themselves, their accomplishments, and their religious practices known to the American public. Still, many problems face the Arab American community as a result of the war on terrorism, which continues to single out Arab and Muslim Americans for special scrutiny on the basis of their ethnic and religious backgrounds. While the events of recent years have been difficult for the Arab American community, they have also led to awareness of the many ways that Arab Americans have participated in American life and made the country a better place for all Americans.

Notes

Introduction: Who Are the Arab Americans?

1. Steve Tamari, "Who Are the Arabs?" *The Arab World in the Classroom.* Washington, DC: Center for Contemporary Arab Studies, Georgetown University, 1999, p. 1.

Chapter One: The Syrian Pioneers: The First Wave

2. Alixa Naff, *Becoming American: The Early Arab Immigrant Experience.* Carbondale: Southern Illinois University Press, 1985, p. 38.
3. Quoted in Gregory Orfalea, *Before the Flames: A Quest for the History of Arab Americans.* Austin: University of Texas Press, 1988, pp. 62–63.
4. Quoted in Sameer Y. Abraham and Nabeel Abraham, *Arabs in the New World: Studies on Arab-American Communities.* Detroit: Wayne State University Press, 1983, p. 37.
5. Orfalea, *Before the Flames*, pp. 57–58.
6. Quoted in Philip M. Kayal and Joseph M. Kayal, *The Syrian-Lebanese: A Study in Religion and Assimilation.* Boston: Twayne, 1975, p. 62.
7. Quoted in Eric J. Hooglund, ed., *Crossing the Waters: Arabic-Speaking Immigrants to the United States Before 1940.* Washington, DC: Smithsonian Institution Press, 1987, p. 30.
8. Orfalea, *Before the Flames*, p. 63.
9. Evelyn Shakir, *Bint Arab: Arab and Arab American Women in the United States.* Westport, CT: Praeger, 1997, p. 22.
10. Shakir, *Bint Arab*, p. 14.

Chapter Two: Settling and Peddling

11. Quoted in Hoogland, *Crossing the Waters*, p. 18.
12. Quoted in Abraham and Abraham, *Arabs in the New World*, p. 16.
13. Quoted in Barbara C. Aswad, ed., *Arabic Speaking Communities in American Cities.* New York: Center for Migration Studies of New York and the Association of Arab-American University Graduates, 1974, p. 28.
14. Quoted in Orfalea, *Before the Flames*, p. 77.
15. Quoted in Abraham and Abraham, *Arabs in the New World*, p. 16.
16. Quoted in Shakir, *Bint Arab*, p. 35.
17. Quoted in Shakir, *Bint Arab*, p. 37.
18. Quoted in Shakir, *Bint Arab.* p. 47.
19. Orfalea, *Before the Flames*, p. 95.
20. Quoted in Hoogland, *Crossing the Waters*, p. 50.
21. Quoted in Ernest McCarus, ed., *The Development of Arab-American Identity.* Ann Arbor: University of Michigan Press, 1994, p. 34.

Chapter Three: Turmoil in the Middle East: The Second Wave

22. Don Peretz, *The Middle East Today.*

Westport, CT: Praeger, 1994, p. 307.

23. Quoted in McCarus, *The Development of Arab-American Identity*, p. 96.

24. Quoted in Munir Akash and Khaled Mattawa, eds., *Post Gibran Anthology of New Arab American Writing.* Syracuse, NY: Syracuse University Press, 1999, p. 359.

25. Edward W. Said, *Out of Place: A Memoir.* New York: Random House, 1999, p. 36.

26. "Palestinian-Born Author Talks of His Life in the United States," *Washington File*, April 3, 2002. http://usinfo.state.gov.

27. Quoted in McCarus, *The Development of Arab-American Identity*, p. 91.

28. Quoted in Orfalea, *Before the Flames*, p. 189.

29. Quoted in Orfalea, *Before the Flames*, p. 180.

30. Erika Kinetz, "Muffled Voices," *New York Times*, March 23, 2003.

31. Quoted in Abraham and Abraham, *Arabs in the New World*, p. 23.

32. Michael W. Suleiman, ed., *Arabs in America: Building a New Future.* Philadelphia: Temple University Press, 1999, p. 10.

Chapter Four: Old Roots, New Branches: Arab Religions in America

33. Quoted in Abraham and Abraham, *Arabs in the New World*, p. 53.

34. Quoted in James Zogby, ed., *Taking Root, Bearing Fruit: The Arab-American Experience.* Washington, DC: American-Arab Anti-Discrimination Committee, 1984, pp. 134–35.

35. Quoted in Abraham and Abraham, *Arabs in the New World*, p. 74.

36. Quoted in Abraham and Abraham, *Arabs in the New World*, p. 73.

37. Quoted in Baha Abu-Laban and Michael W. Suleiman, eds., *Arab Americans: Continuity and Change.* Belmont, MA: Association of Arab-American University Graduates, 1989, p. 74.

38. Quoted in Abu-Laban and Suleiman, *Arab Americans: Continuity and Change*, p. 75.

39. Quoted in "Ramadan USA," *Saudi Aramco World*, January/February 2002, p. 51.

40. Somini Sengupta, "At Holidays, Muslims Find Tests of Patience; Seeking to Keep Hold of Traditions in Land Where Christmas Dominates," *New York Times*, December 25, 1997.

41. Abraham and Abraham, *Arabs in the New World*, p. 166.

42. Johanna Neuman, "The Middle East; Palestinians in U.S. Lament the Unheard Side in the Conflict," *Los Angeles Times*, April 19, 2002, p. A12.

43. Shakir, *Bint Arab*, p. 170.

44. Shakir, *Bint Arab*, pp. 173–74.

Chapter Five: Working in America: All Walks of Life

45. Quoted in "Personality: James Abourezk," *Washington Report*, September 6, 1982, p. 8. www.washington-report.org.

Chapter Six: Finding a Voice

46. James J. Zogby, "Are Arab Americans 'People Like Us'?" *Foreign Service*,

May 2000, p. 34.

47. Quoted in Shakir, *Bint Arab*, p. 176.

48. Quoted in Bushra Karaman and Marvin Wingfield, "Arab Stereotypes and American Educators," *Social Studies and the Young Learner*, March/April 1995, p. 7.

49. Quoted in Karaman and Wingfield, "Arab Stereotypes and American Educators," p. 7.

50. Lerry Ekin and Leila Gorchev, eds., *1991 Report on Anti-Arab Hate Crimes: Political and Hate Violence Against Arab-Americans.* Washington, DC: American-Arab Anti-Discrimination Committee, 1992.

51. Quoted in Ekin and Gorchev, *1991 Report on Anti-Arab Hate Crimes*, p. 8.

52. Quoted in "Arab-Americans Thrive in Detroit," *Christian Science Monitor*, March 15, 1993.

53. Quoted in Jacques Steinberg, "As War Starts, Refugees Feel a Mixture of Dread and Relief," *New York Times*, March 20, 2003, p. A21.

54. Zogby, *Taking Root, Bearing Fruit*, p. 11.

55. Quoted in Carlos Sanchez, "Sentiments from Middle East Resound on the Home Front," *Washington Post*, January 19, 1991.

56. Quoted in Sanchez, "Sentiments from Middle East."

Chapter Seven: Facing the Future

57. Quoted in John Marlowe and Kathleen Burke, "New Stamp Celebrates Eid," *Saudi Aramco World*, September/October 2001, p. 6.

58. ADC, "ADC Condemns Attack on Trade Center, Government Buildings," September 11, 2001. www.adc.org.

59. Quoted in "Arab American, Muslim American Groups Support Anti-Terrorism Campaign," *Washington File*, September 28, 2001. http://usinfo. state.gov.

60. Quoted in "Voices: Brooklyn Arab-Americans Remember September 11," *Saudi Aramco World*, November/ December 2001, p. 4.

61. "Arab and Muslim Americans Offer Key Skills to the Nation," *Washington File*, September 19, 2001. http://usinfo. state.gov.

62. Quoted in "FBI Director Mueller Thanks American Muslim Community," *Washington File*, June 28, 2002. http://usinfo.state.gov.

63. Quoted in Keith Bradsher, "After the Attack: Voices; Shock and Anger Among Arab-Americans," *New York Times*, September 13, 2001.

64. Quoted in "Arab-American, Samar Ali, Urged Community to 'Come Together' After 9/11," *Washington File*, June 28, 2002. http://usinfo.state.gov.

65. Michael S. Lee, *Healing the Nation: The Arab American Experience After September 11.* Washington, DC: Arab American Institute, 2002, p. 7.

66. Quoted in "Remarks at the Islamic Center, Washington, D.C.," *Washington File*, http://usinfo. state.gov.

67. Quoted in Gustave Niebuhr, "Clergy of Many Faiths Answer Tragedy's Call," *New York Times*, September 15, 2001.

68. Quoted in Rachel L. Swarns and Christopher Drew, "Fearful, Angry, or Confused, Muslim Immigrants Register," *New York Times*, April 25, 2003.

69. Rachel L. Swarns, "At Least Thirteen Thousand Arabs and Muslims in U.S. Face Deportation," *International Herald Tribune*, June 9, 2003, p. 7.

70. Sam Dillon, "Suddenly, a Seller's Market for Arabic Studies," *New York Times*, March 19, 2003, p. B7.

71. Quoted in James Oseland, "Lessons from a Muslim Mom," *Rosie* Magazine, February 2002. www.rosie magazine.com.

72. Quoted in Steinberg, "As War Starts, Refugees Feel a Mixture of Dread and Relief."

73. Jodi Wilgoren and Nick Madigan, "Iraqis in U.S. Prepare to Return and Rebuild Homeland," *New York Times*, April 11, 2003, p. B11.

74. Quoted in "Powell Confers with Arab-American Leaders," *Washington File*, June 11, 2002. http://usinfo.state.gov.

FOR FURTHER READING

Books

Anan Ameri and Dawn Ramey, eds., *Arab American Encyclopedia*. Detroit: Gale Group, 2000. A compendium of articles on all aspects of Arab American life, written for use in schools.

Alixa Naff, *The Arab Americans*. Philadelphia: Chelsea House, 1999. A history of Arab Americans with a focus on the Syrians of the first wave.

Naomi Shihab Nye, *Habibi*. New York: Simon & Schuster, 1997. A novel in which an American-born girl visits her relatives on the West Bank.

————, *Words Under the Words: Selected Poems*. Portland, OR: Eighth Mountain Press, 1995. Nye draws on her Palestinian American heritage in this collection of poems.

Edward W. Said, *Out of Place: A Memoir*. New York: Random House, 1999. The renowned scholar recounts growing up in Palestine and Egypt and his education in America.

Bob Temple, *The Arab Americans*. Broomall, PA: Mason Crest, 2003. A short and readable overview of the history of Arab Americans.

Periodicals

Arab Americans, *Cobblestone*, May 2002. Selected essays and activities about the Arab American community.

Websites

American-Arab Anti-Discrimination Committee (www.adc.org). This site offers up-to-date information about the Arab American community and its efforts to combat discrimination. It includes a useful essay by Louise Cainkar, "The History of Arab Immigration to the U.S.: An Introduction for High School Students."

Arab-American Business, 2000–2002 (www.arabamericanbusiness.com). News about prominent Arab Americans in the business world.

Arab American Institute (www.aaiusa.org). Provides a wealth of information about Arab Americans, recent polls of Arab American opinion on a variety of issues, and position papers on recent issues.

Café Arabica: The Arab American Online Community Center (www.cafe arabica.com). A compendium of reprinted articles about the Arab American community.

Council on Islamic Education (www.cie.org). Materials on teaching about Islam, including guides to Islamic holidays.

Washington File (http://usinfo. state.gov). A website of the U.S. Department of State with reports on the Middle East and Islam in America.

Washington Report (www.unausa.org). The *Washington Report* is the publication of the United Nations Association of the United States of America and the Business Council for the United Nations. Provides recent updates of news about the Middle East.

Internet Sources

George W. Bush, remarks at the Islamic Center, Washington, D.C., *Washington File*. http://usinfo.state.gov.

Detroit Free Press, "100 Questions and Answers About Arab Americans." www.freep.com.

Ghada H. Elnajjar, "Powell Confers with Arab-American Leaders," *Washington File*, June 11, 2002. http://usinfo.state.gov.

Philip Kurata, "Arab American, Muslim American Groups Support Anti-Terrorism Campaign," *Washington File*, September 28, 2001. http://usinfo.state.gov.

Robert S. Mueller, "FBI Director Mueller Thanks American Muslim Community," *Washington File*, June 28, 2002. http://usinfo.state.gov.

James Oseland, "Lessons from a Muslim Mom," *Rosie* Magazine, February 2002. www.rosiemagazine.com.

Vicki Silverman, "Arab and Muslim Americans Offer Key Skills to the Nation," *Washington File*, September 19, 2001. http://usinfo.state.gov.

Washington File, "Arab-American, Samar Ali, Urged Community to 'Come Together' After 9/11," June 28, 2002. http://usinfo.state.gov.

———, "Palestinian-Born Author Talks of His Life in the United States," April 3, 2002. http://usinfo.state.gov.

WORKS CONSULTED

Books

James G. Abourezk, *Advise and Dissent: Memoirs of South Dakota and the U.S. Senate.* Chicago: Lawrence Hill Books, 1989. The former senator and founder of the American-Arab Anti-Discrimination Committee remembers his coming of age and years in the Senate.

Sameer Y. Abraham and Nabeel Abraham, *Arabs in the New World: Studies on Arab-American Communities.* Detroit: Wayne State University Press, 1983. These essays provide an overview of the Arab American experience, especially in Detroit.

Baha Abu-Laban and Michael W. Suleiman, eds., *Arab Americans: Continuity and Change.* Belmont, MA: Association of Arab-American University Graduates, 1989. Focuses on Arab American identity, including the role of artists and activists.

Leila Ahmed, *A Border Passage: From Cairo to America—a Woman's Journey.* New York: Penguin, 1999. Writing from the perspective of a Muslim woman, this Harvard professor describes why she grew disenchanted with her life in Cairo.

Munir Akash and Khaled Mattawa, eds., *Post Gibran Anthology of New Arab American Writing.* Syracuse, NY: Syracuse University Press, 1999. Poems, stories, and essays by contemporary Arab American authors.

Barbara C. Aswad, ed., *Arabic Speaking Communities in American Cities.* New York: Center for Migration Studies of New York and the Association of Arab-American University Graduates, 1974. A selection of essays on the Arab American experience in a variety of cities.

Kathleen Benson and Philip M. Kayal, eds., *A Community of Many Worlds: Arab Americans in New York City.* New York: Museum of the City of New York/Syracuse University Press, 2002. A collection of essays that focus on early Arab immigration to New York City and its legacy today.

Larry Ekin and Leila Gorchev, eds., *1991 Report on Anti-Arab Hate Crimes: Political and Hate Violence Against Arab-Americans.* Washington, DC: American-Arab Anti-Discrimination Committee, 1992. A chronology of hate crimes with background information and discussion.

Abdo A. Elkholy, *The Arab Moslems in the United States: Religion and Assimilation.* New Haven, CT: College and University Press, 1966. The author contrasts two Muslim communities, that of Toledo, Ohio, and Detroit, Michigan.

Eric J. Hooglund, ed., *Crossing the Waters: Arabic-Speaking Immigrants to the United States Before 1940.* Washington, DC: Smithsonian Institution Press, 1987. An overview of Arab immigration followed by studies of specific communities and individuals.

———, *Taking Root: Arab-American Community Studies*, vol. 2. Washington, DC: American-Arab Anti-Discrimination Committee, 1985. A look at Arab American communities from Mississippi to Michigan.

Albert Hourani, *A History of the Arab Peoples.* New York: Warner Books, 1991. An overview of the history of the Arab world, its peoples, and cultures.

Hussein Ibish, ed., *1998–2000 Report on Hate Crimes and Discrimination Against Arab Americans.* Washington, DC: American-Arab Anti-Discrimination Committee, 2001. Hate crimes and discriminatory practices, organized in categories including the media, the workplace, and education.

Philip M. Kayal and Joseph M. Kayal, *The Syrian-Lebanese: A Study in Religion and Assimilation.* Boston: Twayne, 1975. This study focuses on the ways in which religion both helped and hindered the assimilation of Arab Christians into the American mainstream.

Michael S. Lee, *Healing the Nation: The Arab American Experience After September 11.* Washington, DC: Arab American Institute, 2002. Arab American responses to the September 11 attacks, and civil rights issues in the wake of events.

Ernest McCarus, ed., *The Development of Arab-American Identity.* Ann Arbor: University of Michigan Press, 1994. This anthology focuses on the early Arab experience in America, ethnic stereotypes, and Arab American identity.

Alixa Naff, *Becoming American: The Early Arab Immigrant Experience.* Carbondale: Southern Illinois University Press, 1985. A book that focuses on the acculturation of the first wave of Syrian immigrants.

Gregory Orfalea, *Before the Flames: A Quest for the History of Arab Americans.* Austin: University of Texas Press, 1988. Orfalea contrasts the early immigrants with second and third wave immigrants who have fled the Arab world in the wake of events since the establishment of Israel and civil war in Lebanon.

Don Peretz, *The Middle East Today.* Westport, CT: Praeger, 1994. A user-friendly textbook that covers the history of the modern Middle East country by country.

Evelyn Shakir, *Bint Arab: Arab and Arab American Women in the United States.* Westport, CT: Praeger, 1997. The experience of Arab American women, including interviews.

Michael W. Suleiman, ed., *Arabs in America: Building a New Future.* Philadelphia: Temple University Press, 1999. A collection of twenty essays on a variety of sociological topics, including political activism and identity.

Teaching About Islam and Muslims in the Public School Classroom: A Handbook for Educators. 3rd ed. Fountain Valley, CA: Council on Islamic Education, 1998. A reference guide to Islam and Muslim students, with a useful glossary.

James Zogby, ed., *Taking Root, Bearing Fruit: The Arab-American Experience.* Washington, DC: American-Arab Anti-Discrimination Committee, 1984. Arab American communities remember their past histories.

Periodicals

Robert Berg and Rick Rickman, "Camels West," *Saudi Aramco World,* May/June 2002.

Keith Bradsher, "After the Attacks: Voices; Shock and Anger Among Arab Americans,"

New York Times, September 13, 2001.

Christian Science Monitor, "Arab-Americans Thrive in Detroit but Stigma from Mideast Conflicts and Terrorism Spark Conflict as Citizens Reach for Mainstream," March 15, 1993.

Adam Clymer, "Government Openness at Issue as Bush Holds On to Records," *New York Times*, January 3, 2003.

Sam Dillon, "Suddenly, a Seller's Market for Arabic Studies," *New York Times*, March 19, 2003.

Patrick Healy, "American Muslims Are Striving for Greater Voice in Politics," *International Herald Tribune*, June 17, 2003.

Bushra Karaman and Marvin Wingfield, "Arab Stereotypes and American Educators," *Social Studies and the Young Learner*, March/April 1995.

Piney Kesting and Robert Azzi, "A Community of Arab Music," *Saudi Aramco World*, September/October 2002.

Omar Khalidi, "Import, Adapt, Innovate: Mosque Design in the United States," *Saudi Aramco World*, November/December 2001.

Erika Kinetz, "Muffled Voices," *New York Times*, March 23, 2003.

John Marlowe and Kathleen Burke, "New Stamp Celebrates Eid," *Saudi Aramco World*, September/October 2001.

Johanna Neuman, "The Middle East; Palestinians in the U.S. Lament the Unheard Side in the Conflict," *Los Angeles Times*, April 19, 2002.

Gustave Niebuhr, "Clergy of Many Faiths Answer Tragedy's Call," *New York Times*, September 15, 2001.

Matthew Purdy, "Watching God and Bush in Patterson," *New York Times*, March 19, 2003.

Carlos Sanchez, "Sentiments from Middle East Resound on the Home Front; Arab American Communities Display Deep Divisions over Persian Gulf War," *Washington Post*, January 19, 1991.

Saudi Aramco World, "Ramadan USA," January/February 2002.

———, "Voices: Brooklyn Arab-Americans Remember September 11," November/December 2001.

Somini Sengupta, "At Holidays, Muslims Find Tests of Patience; Seeking to Keep Hold of Traditions in Land Where Christmas Dominates," *New York Times*, December 25, 1997.

Philip Shenon and David Johnston, "Seeking Terrorist Plots, the FBI Is Tracking Hundreds of Muslims," *New York Times*, October 6, 2002.

Molly Sinclair, "Arab Americans Decry Gulf-Related Harassment; Anti-Discrimination Resolutions Sought," *New York Times*, January 28, 1991.

Jacques Steinberg, "As War Starts, Refugees Feel a Mixture of Dread and Relief," *New York Times*, March 20, 2003.

Rachel L. Swarns, "At Least Thirteen Thousand Arabs and Muslims in U.S. Face Deportation," *International Herald Tribune*, June 9, 2003.

Rachel L. Swarns and Christopher Drew, "Fearful, Angry, or Confused, Muslim Immigrants Register," *New York Times*, April 25, 2003.

Steve Tamari, "Who Are the Arabs?" *The Arab World in the Classroom*. Washington, DC.: Center for Contemporary Arab Studies, Georgetown University, 1999.

Daniel J. Wakin, "Fear for a Navy Son, and for Fellow Muslims," *New York Times*, April 12, 2003.

Louis Werner, "Arab Pop on the World Stage," *Saudi Aramco World*, March/April 2000.

———, "A Gift of Ghazals," *Saudi Aramco World*, July/August 2001.

Jodi Wilgoren and Nick Madigan, "Iraqis in U.S. Prepare to Return and Rebuild Homeland, *New York Times*, April 11, 2003.

James J. Zogby, "Are Arab Americans 'People Like Us'?" *Foreign Service*, May 2000.

Muslims. *See* Islam
Mustafa, Saade, 65, 84

Nader, Ralph, 64, 66
Naff, Alixa, 44
   on Immigration Act of 1924,
     31
   labor and, 24, 27, 30
   Syrians and, 11–12
Naff Arab American Collection,
   79
Nasser, Ahmed, 84
Nasser, Gamal, 33, 44
Nasser, Jacques, 28, 69
National Association of Arab
   Americans (NAAA), 72
National Public Radio, 92
newspapers, 30
New York City, 23–24, 56
   religion and, 47–48
   September 11, 2001, and,
     83–85
New York Times (newspaper), 42,
   53, 79, 89, 91, 94–95
Nye, Naomi Shihab, 62

Oakar, Mary Rose, 75
Oklahoma City bombing, 80
Oman, 7
Orfalea, Gregory, 17, 19, 62, 69
Orientalism (Said), 61
Ottoman Empire, 7
   economic issues of, 10–13
   European intervention and,
     15–16, 32
   extent of, 11
   military draft and, 13
   political oppression and,
     13–14
   religion and, 13–17
   Syrians and, 10
   World War I and, 14, 22, 32
Out of Place (Said), 37

Palestine, 10
   Britain and, 15
   division of, 36
Palestinia Liberation Front, 71
Palestine Liberation
   Organization, 75

Palestinians, 7
   assimilation rates of, 53
   citizenship rights and, 34
   Israeli politics and, 73
   mandate on, 34
   refugees and, 34–38, 54
   self-identity and, 35
   war and, 35, 43
Pan American Airlines, 68–69
Pan-Arabism, 33, 40, 43–44
Paterson Poetry Prize, 62
Pearl Harbor, 90
peddling, 23–28
Peretz, Don, 34
Persian Gulf War, 42, 65, 91
   Arab advocacy and, 76–77,
     80–81
   hate crimes and, 77–78
poetry, 62
politics, 13
   activists and, 64
   Arab Americans in, 63–64
   bias in, 73–76
   disillusionment over, 40–42
   immigration and, 22–23,
     31–32, 38, 40, 61
   mandates, 32, 34
   Palestine division and, 36
   refugees and, 33–38
   religion and, 14–17
   September 11, 2001, and,
     86–88
   special interest groups and, 73
pope, 46
Powell, Colin, 95
Prophet, The (Kahlil Gibran), 61
Protestantism, 12
Puschart Prize, 62

Qatar, 7
al-Qaeda, 93
quiblah (prayer wall), 48

racial profiling, 88–90
radio, 92
rai (music genre), 68
Ramadan (Muslim holiday),
   51–53
Rashid, Stanley, 56
Reagan, Ronald, 63, 71, 74–75

refugees, 33, 34, 36–38
   camps for, 34–35
   citizenship rights and, 34
   detaining of, 34–35, 90
   self-identity and, 35
   support of, 44
   war and, 35, 43
religion, 6
   adaptation of, 47–50
   civil war and, 43
   conflict over, 14–17
   conformity and, 45
   cultural preservation and, 29,
     31
   dating and, 55–56
   Eastern vs. Western, 46
   employment and, 24
   European intervention and,
     15–16
   freedom of worship and, 43
   identity issues and, 47–48
   marriage patterns and, 54–55
   military draft and, 13
   mosques and, 48–49
   September 11, 2001, and, 83,
     85–86
   social status and, 46–48
   see also Christian Arabs;
     Islam
restaurants, 26
Rotary clubs, 63, 91

Saad, Mary, 64
saalam (peace), 18
Said, Edward, 37, 41, 60–61
Salem, George R., 95
Saliba, Najib E., 14
San Joaquin Valley, 60
Saudi Arabia, 7, 48, 88
Saudi Aramco World (magazine),
   65, 84
schools. *See* education
Schur, Joan Brodsky, 112
science, 61, 69
"Sea of Darkness, The." *See*
   Atlantic Ocean
Sengstock, Mary C., 26
September 11, 2001
   Arab culture interest and, 92
   condemnation of, 83

PICTURE CREDITS

ABOUT THE AUTHOR

Joan Brodsky Schur is an educational consultant, author, and teacher. She is coauthor of *In a New Land: An Anthology of Immigrant Literature* and a regular contributor to *Social Education* and other professional journals. Ms. Schur has worked for both the National Archives and PBS Online developing lessons for their websites. She currently serves on the TeacherSource Advisory Group for PBS Online and as social studies curriculum consultant to the Village Community School in New York City, where she has taught English and social studies for over twenty years.